For Pete,
Best Wis...

YO-EKP-838

Hunting
Ducks
and
Geese

A guide to hunting waterfowl
on California's public areas

by Rich Fletcher

2/27/95
...to
CWA CONV '95

Towhee Publishing, Livermore, California

Acknowledgments

I sincerely doubt that it is humanly possible to write a book without the help of your friends. My parents, Nelson and Betty Fletcher, have contributed well beyond the call of duty. My brother Rob and his wife Tish have contributed, especially by being my hunting partners.

I'd also like to thank friends who unselfishly contributed their time to help complete the effort.

Much time, effort and valuable information has been contributed by John and Avis Cowan, Bill Fischer, Ray Burmaster, Dennis Ludington, Dan Chapin, Dick Daniels, Dan Connelly, Bruce Duel, Jerry Cawthon, Ron Cole, Barbara Moy, Marie Salleme, Ralph and Kathy Laughlin, Fred Hilke, Larry DiPietro, Bob Donlan, Chuck Hurley, Barbara Adams, Don Taylor, Sukey Richard, Davina Mayfield, Sharon Cozette, Mac Smith, Margerie Kelly, Bob Johnson, Melba and Kay Weigle.

Thanks go to the many people at the California Department of Fish and Game as well as the United States Fish and Wildlife Service whose cooperation was imperative.

I'd also like to thank CWA and DU for their support.

I must also add that I've enjoyed many new aquaintances in the book publishing industry.

Hunting Ducks and Geese.

Copyright © 1987 by Rich Fletcher.

Printed in the United States of America.

All rights reserved. No part of this book may be used or reproduced in any manor whatsoever without written permission except in the case of brief quotations embodied in critical articles or reviews.

International Standard Book Number: 0-9618844-9-5

For information contact, Towhee Publishing
P.O.Box 8500 #169, Danville, CA 94526

Cover photo courtesy of John B. Cowan

Foreword

This book fills a void that has long existed in the general public's understanding of the opportunities and experiences of waterfowl hunting on public areas. Rich Fletcher not only tells us how to go about hunting on state and federal areas, but he also takes us there through his own recent experiences.

Waterfowl hunting on public areas has matured considerably since its beginnings in the early 1940s. Presently, there are over twenty major public hunting areas in California. In addition, many other public land areas provide minor waterfowl hunting.

Better opportunities for public hunting exist today than ever before. While there are more public areas available to hunters, there are about fifty percent fewer duck hunters than during the 1950s and 1960s. Facilities and techniques for management of hunters and hunting areas have also improved over the years and hopefully further improvements will evolve. Many state and federal wildlife areas have been improving the quality of their wetlands habitat and its diversity. This in turn enhances the hunting experience on these areas.

However, the other side of the coin is that there are fewer birds available on the Pacific Flyway. Even though waterfowl populations are generally higher in California's Central Valley than in other key wintering areas of the nation, California's waterfowl numbers have decreased significantly in recent years. The 1986 U.S. Fish and Wildlife Service-California Department of Fish and Game midwinter aerial survey estimated approximately 3 million ducks and 580,000 geese. This reflects an overall decrease of about thirty percent during the past 12 years. Hence, protection of our vanishing wetlands and waterfowl must continue to be an urgent concern of hunters.

Traditionally, duck hunters have done more than their share to protect the waterfowl resource. They generally contribute more for the preservation, restoration, and maintenance of our marshlands than all other segments of the state's population combined. Hunters pay fees for hunting licenses, state and federal duck stamps, and hunting privileges on wildlife areas. They pay federal taxes on arms and ammunition under the Wildlife Restoration Act. The federal aid to Wildlife Restoration Act alone provides 75 percent of the operational cost of all the state wildlife areas.

Duck hunters also give strong financial support to private-conservation organizations such as Ducks Unlimited and the

California Waterfowl Association. In California alone, Ducks Unlimited raised over four million dollars in 1986 for waterfowl restoration activities.

Rich Fletcher's book serves as a timely reminder of the great outdoor experience provided by hunting. For truly, the hunting experience has more rewards for the hunter than just the birds bagged for consumption. Marshlands are alive with a wide variety of nontarget wildlife and their sounds. To see, to respect, to enjoy, and to appreciate all of the diverse marshlands ecology while hunting is the mark of the true outdoorsman. Most areas maintain sanctuaries, with visitors routes, where large concentrations of birds may be observed. These routes provide a bonus opportunity to view waterfowl in large concentrations.

Waterfowl are public property, to be preserved and managed under the pubic trust. If we wish to continue to enjoy the type of experiences related by Rich Fletcher, we must renew our diligence in upholding that public trust.

John B. Cowan
Wildlife Biologist

Manager, Gray Lodge Wildlife Area
1947-1980

Table of Contents

"...the hunter who accepts the sporting code of ethics keeps his commandments in the greatest solitude, with no witnesses or audience other than the sharp peaks of the mountain, the roaming cloud, the stern oak, the trembling juniper, and the passing animal."

Jose' Ortega y Gasset
philosopher

"A peculiar virtue....is that the hunter ordinarily has no gallery to applaud or disapprove of his conduct. Whatever his acts, they are dictated by his own conscience. .... the ethics of sportsmanship is not a fixed code, but must be formulated and practiced by the individual, with no referee but the Almighty."

Aldo Leopold
conservationist, philosopher

Introduction

What makes a duck so desirable that hunters will expend incredible effort in order to take possession of it? Ducks are so illusive, speedy, and scarce, that they are one of the most sought after game birds. When an attractive outdoor setting is combined with enjoyable camaraderie, the opportunity to observe wildlife, and the bird's great table appeal, you have a sport that can become almost a way of life. The complexity of the pursuit of ducks, which includes the art of calling, decoying, and shooting ducks is addictive to the serious duck hunter. For these reasons, a limit of ducks is a prize held in high regard among those who appreciate the sport and those who hunt the refuges of California make up an important part of this group.

In the 1986–87 duck season, I hunted on eighteen California Wildlife Refuges that are open to controlled duck hunting. The northernmost was Lower Klamath National Wildlife Refuge, and the southernmost was Mendota Wildlife Area. These refuges fall into three categories: national wildlife refuges that are managed by the U.S. Fish and Wildlife Service, national wildlife refuges where the hunting program is managed by the California Department of Fish and Game, and state areas that are managed by the California Department of Fish and Game.

The regulations that govern hunting on these public areas are varied and can be complex. In my discussions of hunting

Hunters at Colusa National Wildlife Refuge, 1952. Photo courtesy of John Cowan.

on the areas, I will discuss regulations. It is important that the hunter read the area regulations before leaving home and to read the information available at the refuges. The rules are frequently revised to meet changing conditions and are strictly enforced.

Why Hunt The Refuges?

The main objective of this book is to encourage hunters to utilize the tremendous hunting resource that exists on the wildlife areas of California. In 1986/87 the number of refuge hunters declined, making opportunities better than in the past. If you already hunt on a wildlife refuge, this book will encourage you to expand your hunting to new areas. By knowing more than one or two areas, opportunities to enjoy good hunting during the premium hunting periods will increase. If you are a novice or a displaced duck hunter, this book will provide the information necessary to make your first hunt on a wildlife area a better experience, and it will speed up the process by which you learn an area intimately. Hunt-

2

ing the refuges is the best way to break into hunting ducks, as it is top quality hunting at an affordable price. If you are a duck hunter who owns duck hunting property or leases a duck blind, you should be able to use the information in this book to expand your opportunities to hunt. Due to the migratory nature of ducks, unreliable water supplies, and variable crop harvest dates, alternative hunting locations are desirable. I would also recommend the book to duck hunting enthusiasts who want to compare their own experiences with mine. It is possible that some of my ideas may be incorporated into other duck hunting situations. I hope that some hunters will enjoy reading about my trips as a substitute for duck hunting, but only when the opportunity to take to the field isn't available.

Before this season, my duck hunting had taken place mainly on our private duck club and one refuge, Kesterson National Wildlife Refuge. As is the case with most refuge duck hunters, I concentrated my efforts on Kesterson because I didn't want to spend a great deal of time investigating new areas. Knowing a refuge well can certainly be advantageous. The hunter with experience on one particular refuge will often have a high rate of success. On the other hand, the value of knowing a refuge is, at times, overrated, and in some cases a dogmatic approach will be a hindrance. One of the objectives of this book is to show the reader techniques that will increase the chance of success on the first hunt of a refuge and it will certainly speed up the process of learning an area. As you continue to read, you will probably find similarities between your own experiences and mine.

The Hunt – In the Field

Overview

When analyzing a refuge duck hunt, it's best to break the hunt down into several important areas of consideration. The first is equipment. Without proper equipment the hunter will fail before reaching the pond. When hunting ducks the hunter must be able to withstand a wide range of weather elements. The weather can range from hot and dry with temperatures in the eighties to miserably cold with temperatures below freezing and the wind blowing forty miles per hour. Without the ability to stay outdoors for long periods of time in all weather conditions, the hunter will be limited and unable to stay in the field during time periods when the chances of success are the greatest. An equipment checklist is provided and a discussion of the equipment that I've used will be given in a later chapter.

The second area of critical importance is location. Which refuge, and where on that refuge, should you hunt? (Choosing which refuge to hunt will be discussed separately.) One can only be successful on a refuge duck hunt if a blind location is secured where the ducks are going to fly by. Ducks are finicky about where they land and will frequent one spot only a few yards from another where they seldom touch down. This is especially true after the shooting starts. In discussions of hunts, I will also talk about the good or poor locations and how I ended up in them. Hopefully, you can take advantage of my experiences. Once the hunter has reached the desired spot, there are a multitude of options available for the set up. Different options will produce results at different times of year and under different weather conditions. In discussions of the hunts made, I will explain why a setup worked or didn't work and why I chose a certain method. Sometimes a variety of methods must be tried until something works. Other times a setup is acceptable, but the timing isn't right. Sometimes, nothing will work. It's these days that provide the

5

ultimate challenge because duck hunting is an art. One never knows when the influences on the ducks will change, making them once again vulnerable to the hunter. The many factors which influence duck behavior create a dynamic situation.

After entering the blind, the hunters' actions in the blind can have a tremendous influence on the behavior of ducks in the area. Moving, shifting, and talking will reduce the hunters' chances for success. Looking upward at ducks that are working a pond, especially late in the season, will often spook a prospective target. There won't be much discussion of these negative influences, but I will try to present some worthwhile discussion of duck calling and how it affected the hunts in which I participated.

Obviously, shooting is a very important part of duck hunting. Marksmanship is important, but nothing outside of practice will improve your shooting ability. Knowing when to shoot, however, is something that influences hunter success just as much as marksmanship and is one area of duck hunting that separates the artisan from the hacker.

Retrieving ducks is the last area of importance in the field. No useful purpose is served by shooting a duck and then leaving it in the marsh. Dogs are important in this part of duck hunting, but on refuges there are many problems created by dog use. I'd prefer not to have one along unless the dog is well trained and I know exactly where I'll be hunting. There are some simple techniques that can be used to reduce the loss of downed ducks, and I'll discuss them in the section on retrieving.

Selecting a Blind and Setting Up

Several key factors should be considered when locating a blind. First of all, a pond must be found that the ducks like. After finding such a pond, a blind must be found so that the hunter can remain unseen as ducks approach. After selecting a blind location, the decoys must be set out in a location where the birds can fly towards them allowing the hunter to have a reasonable chance for a successful shot. Open water,

This photo of Jerry Fawns shows a typical blind used on a wildlife area. Tules are often tall enough for almost total concealment while providing ample visibility. Photo courtesy of John Cowan.

wind direction, and sun direction are the major considerations. In contrast to the club duck hunter, who may have years to study the way that ducks work on a particular pond, the refuge hunter must learn to read a pond quickly and assess its layout in just a few minutes.

What kind of pond should you look for?

When looking for a pond, size is a primary consideration. (Especially if sprig are your number one target.) In general, it pays to start with the largest body of water in the area. Mallards often like small "potholes," and there are good "small ponds" to be found, but it's generally best to start with the largest pond available and then watch to see where the birds work. Sometimes, a pond that looks small will work, especially if it's in the center of a continuous string of small ponds, or if the area hasn't been heavily hunted. Other times the reason why ducks like a pond will be obscure, but the fact that they are there is testimony enough. If you spot ducks working a pond, that is the best evidence that you can get. Once you find a spot that the ducks like, go back to it. Knowing these spots is what sets the successful hunter apart from the rest. Both Dennis Ludington and Ray Burmaster

The hunter's face is easily visible from above. Many hunters use face paint to alleviate this problem. Photo Courtery of John Cowan.

look for ponds with thick growth during windy or cold weather as the birds seek out protection. It might pay to keep this in mind.

Where should the blind be located?

If a very large pond is selected (say over forty acres), set up near the center of the pond or on the up-wind half of the pond. Generally the birds will be high when they pass over the down-wind half of the pond and then they will look for a place to land near the center of the pond or just up-wind of center. It is very difficult to get good shots on the down-wind side of a large pond. It pays to know which direction the winds tend to blow during specific weather situations. On days with similar weather conditions, the ducks will probably be landing in the same spots. In this respect, the refuge duck hunter has a big advantage over the club hunter whose blind is stuck in the same location for all types of weather. The blind should have tules or other vegetation large enough to hide in. Over the course of the 1986–87 season, my most successful hunts were out of tule blinds. I try to hunt from tules whenever possible. A single clump of brush in the center of an otherwise clear pond usually won't work; the ducks will be suspicious of it and shy away, especially if you try to call from it. The blind should be in a location where it is one spot out of many

If you want to hunt pintail, select a spot with as much open water as possible and bring as many decoys as you can. Although they're not California's number one duck anymore, they're still in the top five on most refuges. Photo courtesy of John Cowan.

similar spots. Color of the vegetation can be significant if it doesn't blend with the color of the camouflage being worn by the hunter. The blind should be located in a spot such that the decoys can be placed where the hunter can shoot at birds over the decoys, or just down-wind of them, without looking into the sun. The birds will generally approach the decoys from down-wind and this is fundamental to blind and decoy location. The ducks will also avoid landing while looking into the sun, so the combination of wind and sun may produce a compromise flight direction. The more in-line you are with the path to the decoys, the better the hiding spot must be in order to remain undetected. Sometimes one must compromise some of these elements in setting up due to the unavailability of the perfect spot. It pays to be patient when selecting blind location. Once you are set up, it's a great deal of trouble to pick up and start over again. Sometimes it's best to hunt from a blind for a while before putting out the decoys. By waiting and watching, you get a chance to see how the ducks work the pond and where they want to land. If the birds have an established pattern for how they work the pond, then your decoys will work best if they fit into the normal pattern.

9

About Calling

My theories about duck calling are the result of personal experience and are only one man's opinion, but I'm certain that at least some of what I have to say on the subject is worthwhile. The way that ducks respond to a call is dependent upon the situation in the swamp on any given day. The type of duck being called is very important, but ducks will often come to the call of a different species. The type of duck that is predominant in the area is important and the weather has a big impact on the effectiveness of calling. The time of season is very important in determining the best calling strategy. There are times when calling seems to accomplish nothing.

Should you own a duck call?

In general, the quality of duck calling on the wildlife refuges has improved over what was heard several seasons ago. Give the credit to the improved quality of economical calls and to the high quality instructional tapes that are available. The ability to make the various sounds necessary to attract ducks can be learned at home using instructional tapes and videos. The application of these sounds to the hunting situation is the second phase of duck calling and is critical. When setting up, you should pay attention to other hunters who may be calling in the area. If the guy next to you is continuously blaring away on a mallard call, then you may want to consider finding another location. This is particularly true late in the season when ducks may be especially shy. When I hunt, I like to be calling ducks independent of other hunters. Each type of duck will respond differently to the calls. The mallard call is the most common call used by hunters, but is difficult to master and not as versatile as the sprig and teal whistles. After proficiency is attained, the mallard call is fun to use. Having a duck respond to your call is one of the most satisfying events in duck hunting, so by all means get a mallard call and a sprig whistle. At first, it's probably a good idea to practice in your car, and then on hunts where you have a chance to be on your own. You'll learn faster this way because you won't be embarrassed when you sound bad. The mallard call is most effective during the early season and during times when there are very few hunters in the area. Other ducks will come to a mallard call, especially spoonbill and gadwall. Sprig will come to the mallard call, but not as readily as they will the whistle, so it pays to stick with the whistle when sprig are the prevalent bird in the area. Teal will come readily to almost any whistle and widgeon like the sprig sounds. As a matter of personal preference, I don't generally use the widgeon sounds, but some hunters use the widgeon sounds frequently, and even if you don't shoot widgeon, they still make good decoys for other ducks. The whistle works in most situations, is easy to learn, and is versatile. The hunter next door will appreciate your whistle also.

Weather and calling

In bad weather call often. The mallard call can be used almost continuously during stormy weather, but on still days you should hold the mallard call down to single quacks and a few hails. In clear weather and late in the season when ducks are shy, quit calling while birds are still a ways out as they will spot you if you call from close range. Sometimes, during the early season, you can get away with calling when they're overhead, but be careful, and if you think they may have seen you, they probably did. Sometimes the single quack can get a bird to fly right in on you, and a twenty–five yard shot will result.

Responses to the call

When calling, watch the bird closely and learn to read the bird's response through it's actions. The birds will respond with consistency to your call and certain patterns will result. When a teal or mallard has decided to come to the call you can usually tell that the bird is homing in on you because it will point directly towards you. If it does, stop calling. If the bird veers off, then start calling again but only after you're sure that it won't spot you. Spoonbill, teal, and gadwall will often dive-bomb into your decoys as they respond to the call. When a bird comes in this way, it may pay to stand up a little early and flair the birds, thus creating an easier shot with the ducks climbing. If you don't flair them, they won't slow down until they hit the water. This habit makes them a tough target, even at close range. It's hard to spot the sprig's response to the call. When I call sprig, I generally try to call at a consistent frequency. When sprig are in the area, they seem to be whistling all the time, so don't stop whistling. Try to call as if you are representing a certain number of birds and then stay with that representation until it's time to shoot. Widgeon are similar to sprig in this respect, except that they will almost always come in sooner and with less deliberation. When there are birds in the area, but none are responding, I will try different calls to see what works. This will include periods of no calling at all. There are times when it is best to minimize calling. Occasionally I'll not make a sound until the bird is down low and about ready to land. At this point (if he's not yet in range) a single quack, just loud enough to be heard, can be deadly.

Why is calling on a refuge different from on a club?

One of the major differences between calling ducks during a refuge hunt (compared to a club hunt), is that during a refuge hunt, you'll probably be hunting from a temporary blind which doesn't provide absolute concealment. For this reason you must be extra cautious about calling when the birds are close-in or overhead. From a well concealed barrel blind, I call more frequently while the birds are working than I do from a tule blind. Keep this in mind when you listen to instructors and their instructional tapes, as they are generally hunting out of well concealed permanent blinds and assume that the listener is also.

Is a goose call important?

Goose calling is a whole new ball game. In most refuge

hunting situations, with the exception of the Canada goose (honkers), the goose call is unimportant. Although snow geese are successfully hunted on refuges, it's a rare day when a snow goose can be called in. The tendency for the snow goose to stay in large groups and "follow the leader" makes it a difficult bird to influence. The Canada goose is much more susceptible to the call. Nearly all of the honkers that I've shot or shot at have been influenced by calling. Honkers will respond to the call from long distances, and will fly directly into the call. Once again learning to make the sound is only the first step. As with duck calling, the general trend is to call less frequently as the birds approach. Like mallards and teal, the Canada goose will tend to "lock on" at some point. When this response is noticed, the main thing to do is get ready to shoot and then remain as still as possible. I've been advised to keep one hand on the gun and the other on the call in case they start to change course. This makes sense. The white front goose (specklebelly) may respond to many different calls, even the mallard call. The spec will sometimes fly directly into the call and other times work in gradually. Either the honker call or snow goose call may work. Some of the calls designed specifically for white fronts can also be used for snow geese.

When to Shoot

Selecting shots is an area of duck hunting which I consider to be the big downfall for most hunters. Ducks can be killed at ranges up to eighty yards. Almost everybody has, at one time or another, pulled up on a duck that seemed to be out of range, and shot it dead. There is a tendency to think that once a shot is accomplished, it should be tried again. There is also the desire to fire test shots.

When is the bird in range?
There are a number of reasons why the duck hunter is better off not shooting long shots. Reducing the range at which one shoots, increases success and enjoyment. It is a step towards

Selecting drakes forces the shooter to concentrate on one bird, which prevents "flock shooting." Photo courtesy of John Cowan.

a better understanding of ducks, and helps improve the relationship between hunters in the field. While considering whether or not to shoot at a duck, there are other considerations besides range. Ducks fly at many different speeds as they approach decoys, most hunters figure that any time a duck is within range, it is in their best interest to shoot. It is my opinion that it is in the hunter's best interest to shoot only shots for which he is mentally and physically prepared to shoot. If for any reason the hunter is not prepared to shoot at a bird (with the idea that he **should** hit it), then it is in the hunter's best interest to pass up the shot. I base this theory on the fact that, on any given day the hunter will get a limited number of chances to shoot ducks. Each time the hunter shoots, the area is rid of any working ducks and essentially, the process of attracting birds starts over again from scratch. On the other hand, if the shot is passed up, it is likely that the same bird will come back for another shot opportunity. Even if the bird doesn't return, there are often other birds working that will come in as long as the hunter hasn't shot. Whenever one bird has reached the decoys, then another is probably right behind it. There is no better decoy than a live duck flying over your decoys!

Picking out which duck to shoot

My brother, Rob, and I hunt with our friend Fred quite often, and its no secret among the members of our group that Fred has a knack for picking out his birds. If a flock comes over, Fred always picks out a hen. I don't know exactly how he does it, because the odds are against him. There are more drakes than hens. I can't recall seeing two or more ducks together when at least one wasn't a drake. I seldom shoot a hen. (I'm speaking primarily of mallards and sprig, but it doesn't hurt to treat other species with the same respect.) I'm not saying this to impress anybody; I'm saying it to give you confidence that shooting only drakes, will not reduce the number of ducks you take home. Avoiding needless killing of hens is good for the ducks and it improves your skills as a duck hunter. When you watch ducks, always pick out the drakes, even if you're not shooting. It is a skill that will improve with time. You'll be surprised how quickly you'll reach the point where you seldom kill a hen. It is Rob's opinion that shooting only drakes has made him a better shot by preventing flock shooting. I also find that if I can't spot the drakes, they're not in range yet!

When to pass shoot

There are occasions when ducks will not work decoys. If this is the case, it may be necessary to pass shoot in order to have a chance at ducks. (I would define pass shooting as shooting at birds that are not intending to land in the vicinity of the hunter but happen to fly over on their way to some other location.) Every effort should be made to decoy ducks before pass shooting, and then the hunter must decide if he wants to be a pass shooter. Pass shooting at ducks is an entirely different form of duck hunting from decoy hunting. The state of mind that the hunter is in while pass shooting is no closer to decoy shooting than is skull boating. The pass shooter and decoy hunter must share the same refuge. It is my opinion that the pass shooter has an obligation to other hunters on the refuge, not to try every conceivable shot with

Dogs must be well trained or they can cause a multitude of problems. This dog, "Thor" posed at field trials in 1978. Photo courtesy of John Cowan.

the idea that the duck might be in range. Essentially, the guys who hunt refuges are partners in the same duck club and the success of each hunter is the success of all. Unfortunately, not all hunters feel this way. One hunter told me that he could hit ducks at eighty yards, so for him it was okay to shoot the long shots. He credited his success on long shots to "hot loads." He'll be upset when he hunts next to the guy that thinks his "hot loads" can kill ducks at a hundred yards.

There are locations on some refuges that are ideal for pass shooting. There are "firing lines" on several refuges where hunters do nothing but pass shoot. Snow geese in particular are difficult to have a chance at unless you pass shoot. I've had hunters tell me about good pass shooting opportunities at almost every refuge. I seldom hunt with the intention of pass shooting, but one of the keys to success is the same as with decoy hunting– observation. Observation will lead you to places where the geese or ducks are flying on a particular day. The combination of wind and the location where the birds have landed will result in a flyway where the birds will repeatedly fly over. This is usually long–range shooting and takes a special knack for the long lead. Each hunter is out on the refuge for a unique reason, and you need to decide what you're there for. If you don't like carrying decoys and if you're not interested in calling, but you like the challenge of shooting long ranges and the anticipation that comes with watching your target coming for a long way, then maybe pass shooting is for you.

Retrieving

Once the duck is hit, somebody must keep his eyes on the bird until it is lying dead on the water. In some cases, it is acceptable to see that a duck is dead in the air over open water. Especially in the case of the independent hunter, it is usually necessary to forsake shooting at a second bird if the first bird is hit. Trying to shoot doubles more often than not leads to lost birds. Whenever you take your eyes off a bird that has been hit, a number of things can go wrong. It can start to fly again, it can swim away, or you may spin around and loose track of where it went down. If a bird is on the water, and it is alive, I generally shoot it again. Several times I have seen a duck get away when it seemed as if there was no route of escape. Once this last season, I walked up to a downed honker that had been hit several times and it took off as though it were perfectly healthy. Several times in the past I have seen ducks escape that appeared to be dead.

Marking the bird's location
If a bird goes down at a distance, and is so far away that you can't see it hit the water, then the line of sight to the bird is critical. I generally try to go directly to the bird without taking my eyes off the line to it. If you must take your eyes off that

Junior license holders enter the refuge at no charge and each reservation can admit two adults and four juniors. (In order to obtain a junior license, the hunter must be under 16 years of age.) In this photo Randy and Loren Ratterman are shown returning from a successful coot shoot. Photo courtesy of John Cowan.

spot for even just one glance, then make sure that you carefully select some object on the horizon to mark the location. The horizon must be carefully examined to make sure that the spot you pick won't be confused with another when you again look up. Once you are sure of the line of sight, then a duck can be found at a great distance by just following that line. Once you reach the location where you think the bird hit the ground, drop your hat or handkerchief. This will serve as a reference point so that you don't get confused during a lengthy search.

Do you need a dog?

I have a dog that is a mediocre retriever at best, but I sometimes bring her along for company and she sometimes has found birds for me that would have otherwise been lost. A dog creates a multitude of problems when hunting on a refuge. A good dog is invaluable when it comes to retrieving ducks; a bad dog is another story. If you're a "full-time" duck hunter, then get a good dog and train him properly. If for some reason you don't have a dog, don't worry about it. Be careful with your shooting and you'll get most of the birds that you hit. The problems encountered with dogs include: fighting with other dogs, not staying still in the blind, retrieving other hunters ducks, and disappearing into the dark when going or coming from the field. These problems can be overcome with good training. The number one problem is that you never know if there will be a suitable place for the dog to stay while hunting. I know one duck hunter who says that his dog can swim in three-foot deep water all day while he hunts ducks. That sounds cruel to me, but each dog owner must decide what's best for his own dog. There will be more information on dog use in the interview with Dennis Ludington.

Hunting a Refuge for the First Time

Approaching a refuge with the idea of hunting it for the first time can be a mind boggling experience. Many times I have wandered around in the dark with the feeling that it was necessary to find a good spot before daylight so that I could have a chance during those first few moments after legal shooting time. Many times I have spent an hour putting out decoys in a pond that looked great in the dark. Later, when the sun rose, I would realize that it was too small and poorly situated. The temptation to stick it out to see if maybe some ducks would come in is hard to deny. After several hours of hunting at this inferior location, I'd either become discouraged and leave or sit it out all day figuring that it was just a poor day to hunt ducks. Fortunately, there's a better way.

Heading out in the dark

When hunting unknown areas, I can safely say that I have never discovered a good spot in the dark. I have tried many times, but I've always ended up picking up the decoys and moving in order to find success. Occasionally I've had some luck with good directions from other hunters, but even good directions are a long shot. Once an area is explored and the routes to specific ponds learned, then setting up early in total darkness is an advantage. On first trips in an area, I prefer to head out about shooting time. You can't compete with the regulars, so don't try. Instead, take advantage of the situation and see where the successful hunters are set up. Next time you may get one of these spots. If I do head out in the dark, I'll study the area map and pick out a general area that looks interesting. If the refuge is near its quota of hunters. I'll head for a location at least one mile from the nearest parking lot. This automatically weeds out a large number of the competition. Usually, a light on the horizon or a star can be used as a marker for your heading, but I carry a compass for extra dark or foggy days. It's easy to think that you've gone too far when travelling in the dark, so I count steps to make sure that I'm going as far as it seems. For a ball park estimate I count 2000 steps per mile. After I've walked the desired distance, I then start looking for a large body of water. It's important that the water appears to be quite large because all ponds look larger in the dark than they do in daylight. Several times I've had the sun come up and make me feel foolish. Pond size is critical for drawing ducks. (There are certainly good potholes that may be quite small, but when hunting an area for the first time, you'll be better off if you start out on a good size pond.) In general, you'll also do better if you can find ponds that are permanent. Permanent ponds will have lush growth and will generally be deeper.

Observation, the key to success

Once a pond is selected, the hunter must keep in mind that it is almost impossible to start out at the best spot on the pond. You may find that right next door to you is a spot that the ducks like, so don't put all your decoys out in the dark; wait until you've established the best spot in the general area. After you've seen how the ducks work the area, then put out all your decoys. I carry two large floating goose decoys that are easy to put out and pick up. I'll use the goose decoys first. (During the early season, two magnum mallard decoys would be better.) Once a spot is located where ducks are working, then ten mallard decoys go out. If they're needed and the spot is a good one then the rest of the decoys go out. **In the dark it's usually hard to resist the temptation to put all the decoys out, but it pays to wait.**

What to do if there's no action

If a pond turns out to be a total bust, as is frequently the case, pick up the decoys and look for a new pond. I'll generally wait about an hour before moving. While hunting, watch nearby areas and look and listen for ducks that are working. Hopefully you'll see ducks that fly low over other areas. The pond that they're working may not be visible, but wherever the ducks fly low, there will be a pond. A pair of field glasses comes in handy at this point. On foggy days you may hear birds splashing or calling. It's easiest to let the ducks find your next pond for you. After spotting ducks working, investigate the new area. If you find a spot that looks real good, go ahead and put all the decoys out. If you're still not sure, repeat the initial process. Sometimes it will be necessary to move more than once. As long as too much effort isn't invested in decoys, then the move isn't difficult. There are other variables that can have an effect on the results of this method. If other hunters nearby have a tremendous number of decoys, or if there is a good caller in the area, it may be best to move a long distance from this spot. One of the advantages of walking a long way is that it is difficult for other hunters to carry large numbers of decoys to remote locations. Since road-less areas present a difficult problem for those hunters that carry a large number of decoys, there's an advantage to finding areas with no roads. Large quantities of decoys are hard to compete with, especially late in the season when ducks are shy and looking to raft up with other ducks in protected areas. One aspect of refuge hunting that can be distasteful is competition for birds. Normally it is best to avoid the competitive situation as it will probably reduce the enjoyment of the hunt.

21

The late start

Because of the difficulties involved in heading out onto a new refuge in the dark, I have found that it's often better to wait until light before leaving the parking lot. There are many advantages to arriving at a refuge about a half hour before shooting time. You can usually find out which areas of the refuge are crowded. Avoid them! It's easier to find a good pond after daylight. It's less work if you only put your decoys out once, and it's also easier to avoid other hunters. This approach works quite well on the days when the refuge is not heavily hunted. During mid-season, it is unusual to have any trouble getting into a refuge at shooting time. I was never turned down in 1986-87. (It would pay to keep your eye on shoot reports to see how crowded the refuges have been before you count on making it in this way.)

Afternoon hunt

Another consideration is starting out in the late morning or mid-day period as other hunters are leaving. Its nice to be able to observe hunters to see where the action is. Most hunters pick up before noon, leaving opportunities available to the hunter who observes and then steps into the best areas of the refuges. Several of my best shoots were during the afternoon. A Saturday afternoon shoot can be a good way to locate a spot for Sunday morning. To get your money's worth, buy a season permit. This will allow you to enter the refuge late, without feeling a financial burden. I think this is what makes the season pass so desirable.

What You'll Need To Know Before Leaving Home

Which Public Area Should I Hunt?

The first question that must be answered by each duck hunter before hunting the public areas is: which area should I hunt? Whether you're a first-time duck hunter or a seasoned veteran, the biggest difference between you and the club hunter is that you have a choice. Each time you leave home, various hunting locations and habitat are available to you.

Define your priorities

If you place too much importance on success while making this decision, it could be counter productive. No matter how scientific your approach, nothing will guarantee that the ducks will be at any given place at any particular time, so I'd recommend that you consider many different factors, not all of which have to do with your chance of success. How much time do you have? Which refuges do you know? What time of year is it? How crowded will a particular area be? Where are hunters having the most success? Do you want to have a chance at geese? Do you want to shoot honkers? Do you want to stay in a travel-trailer? Do you want to test out your new skull boat? Is your dog especially susceptible to cold? Do you own decoys? How far can you hike? Do you have a junior hunter with you? Are you handicapped? Do you also want to pheasant hunt or snipe hunt? Do you like to jump shoot? Do you want to hunt out of a permanent barrel blind?

Each hunter must place a personal amount of importance on these factors and come up with the best answer. I can't possibly begin to do that for you, but I will do the best I can to put enough information into this book so you can come out with the answer that will be best for you. These questions are the reason for the book. It will take a lifetime of duck hunting to find some of the answers.

Sources Of Information About Hunter Success

One thing that many hunters like to know is how the refuges are shooting. If an area is hot then some hunters will go to that refuge to take advantage of the greater number of birds in that area. *Western Outdoor News* and *Hunting and Fishing News* publish this information along with other related facts about the refuges. Each week during the year I find good information about waterfowling in these publications. The major newspapers in your area probably publish waterfowl information weekly. The *San Francisco Chronicle* is the paper I most frequently read, and the results are usually in the back of the sports page. I give this information only passing consideration as kill results are not a major factor in my decision where to hunt. Some hunters, (Ray Burmaster for example) use these surveys to decide where to be on any given shoot day. (There is an interview with Ray later in the book.) A friend of mine told my brother that he never went out in 1986 because the published results indicated that the hunting was poor. I'd recommend that you judge the hunting on a more personal basis than that.

Los Banos Wildlife Area offers information by telephone that pertains to hunts at Los Banos, Volta, San Luis, Kesterson, and Merced refuges. Information on the tape includes: special hunts, waterfowl hunting conditions, and shooting results. During the waterfowl season, up-dated results are available at 8:30 a.m. each Monday morning. The phone number is (209) 826-6719.

Regulations

Read the regs

The rules that govern the use of refuges can sometimes be confusing. There are regulations that are unique to each particular area. It pays to read all available information about a refuge before hunting it for the first time in a season. There are three documents that set forth the rules on the refuges. The first is Part III of the hunting regulations. This document defines season bag and possession limits, season dates, and general hunting regulations for the various major areas in the state. The second document is entitled "California Regulations for Hunting on State and Federal Areas." This document describes all of the public hunting areas in the state and the rules governing them. It provides general information such as location, restrictions on the use of boats and or travel-trailers. In addition it defines the procedures that must be followed to gain access and the cost of doing so. Both of these documents are available at local sporting goods dealers. The third document is available only at the hunting area. It consists of an area map and the special rules that apply to that area.

Getting in line

Each refuge will have its own method of assigning hunters a priority for getting into the refuge. This priority list will apply to both non-reservations and reservations. One should always ask about the method of accountability as soon as possible after arriving at the refuge. One space in line can make a difference in where you get to hunt the next day. In my experience I've never been treated unfairly, but you've got to be prepared to stick up for your rights. Keep in mind that on any given day, most of the hunters in line will have hunted that refuge before, and the refuge personnel may assume that everybody understands the system, especially if nobody asks. The best policy is to approach the check–in station and

This information board at Honey Lake Wildlife Area shows some of the restrictions commonly found.

tell the person in charge of the check–in process that you're new at that refuge and you want to make sure you understand the procedure.

Fees

The basic fee to hunt was $10 per day in 1986/87. There was also a two–day and a season pass offered. These prices are bargains for hunters. I don't know of any plans to increase the price in 1987/88. Some of the refuges sell the two day or season passes at the refuges, but, as a general rule, it's best to purchase these at a sporting goods store before you leave home so nothing can go wrong.

The season permit

In 1986/87, a type "A" season permit was offered for $75. The type "A" permit permitted entry onto all areas with no additional charge. A type "B" season permit was issued for access to the northern areas. (Ash Creek, Butte Valley and Honey Lake) For a regular refuge hunter, this was a super bargain. Not only does it cut down the cost per trip, but it

These vehicles are in the non-reservation line at Los Banos Wildlife Area.

removes any stigma attached to a brief hunt. Once you're at the refuge, you might as well go out and shoot at some birds instead of sitting around the parking lot. I started out at 2:30 p.m. a couple of times with the idea that I might learn a little about the area and also get a couple of opportunities to shoot a duck. I probably wouldn't have done this if it had cost me extra.

Reservations

This information is perishable. The procedure used to select reservations is always subject to change. It could change before this book is published.

The proceedure

Ten days before specified shoot days, the California Department of Fish and Game conducts a lottery. The purpose of the lottery is to determine who will be guaranteed entrance to the refuges for that shoot day. In order to enter the lottery hunters must submit request cards. Successful applicants will receive the card back with a validation mark on it. This card becomes a ticket to enter the refuge that was requested. Individual hunters are allowed to submit one card per refuge per hunt day. There are no reservations drawn for Sunday shoots except on the opening weekend, closing weekend, and during the pheasant season for some refuges. (According to Bruce Deuel at the Waterfowl Co-ordinator's Office, this is under consideration for change in 1987/88.) In order to be valid, each card must have a stamp on it. There is a fee charged for the stamp. The purpose of the fee is to produce revenue to cover the cost of conducting the lottery. ($1 in 86/87) The cards can be obtained from license agents along with the stamps.

Should you try for reservations

There are many reasons why you're better off if you have reservations. You know you'll get in. If you get near the front of the reservation line, you can just about pick the spot you want, anywhere on the refuge. (Don't dilly-dally on your way out.) Some people prefer not to have to spend the night at the refuge. Even if you show up at the last minute before the refuge opens to hunters, having reservations guarantees a reasonably early entrance.

What are the odds of getting drawn?

The chances that your card may be drawn on any given shoot day vary greatly. The chances of getting drawn for opening day are slim on any refuge, but during the middle of the season one has a good chance on most refuges. For some refuges, there are times during the season when everybody who submits a reservation card will get drawn. In 1986, I submitted eleven cards and was drawn twice. These submissions were all early in the season and after going to San Luis and Grizzly Island with reservations, I decided that it wasn't important to submit for them any more. I had no trouble getting into the refuges without reservations. Since I was hunting refuges that I'd never seen before, it was best to wait until nearly daylight before heading out anyway. (Also keep in mind that it may not always be so easy. There have been years in the past when the refuges filled regularly all season long.)

The reservation is most advantageous when the hunter knows a really good spot that is popular. By obtaining a reservation and getting to the refuge early, a good location can be secured and success is likely. There are some spots that are so popular that only the very first people in the reservation line get a chance to hunt them. Such is the case with spaced blinds four, five, and six at Los Banos Wildlife Area.

At the northern refuges, only the opening weekend is limited by the reservation requirement. At Tule Lake and Lower Klamath National Wildlife Refuges, requests for opening day must be submitted in August. No hunters are allowed on the refuge without reservations so if you don't get drawn, there's no other way to get in for opening weekend. (The Sheepy units at Lower Klamath and the Panhandle at Tulelake are minor exceptions to this rule, but in most cases, won't offer significant enough hunting opportunity to justify making the trip north.) Other Northeast refuges (Ash Creek, Butte Valley, and Honey Lake) had similar policies towards opening weekend in 1986/87. This isn't true at the Sacramento Valley and San Joaquin Valley refuges where there is a non-reservation line on opening weekend.

Decoys And Decoy Carriers

Selecting proper decoys is a complex problem for the refuge duck hunter. Most decoys are designed to be set in place for the season. Generally, because they are light, the main problem when carrying them is bulk, not weight. Since the refuge duck hunter is not allowed to leave decoys in the field overnight, he must carry them to the hunting location each day. Compromises must be made between decoy appearance, number of decoys, and decoy size. For most hunters, price is also a consideration.

This decoy carrier is loaded for a hunt at Los Banos Wildlife Area.

What kind of decoys are best?

I carry ten standard size hard body mallard decoys. In addition, I have about eighteen inflatable decoys, which are sprig. I sometimes carry rubber decoys that are self–inflating when dropped into the water. These are less bulky, but heavy and less effective. Two large floating snow goose decoys are carried in addition to the duck decoys. They are tied onto the exterior of my backpack. When honker hunting, a dozen honker shells replace the eighteen sprig decoys.

What's the best way to carry decoys?

There are an infinite number of combinations of decoys and ways to carry them. In the refuge situation the hunt is greatly limited, not only by the decoys themselves, but also by the method for getting them into the field. Decoy carriers on wheels greatly increase the number of decoys that can be carried, but when using them there are certain parts of each refuge that cannot be reached. Usually, the decoy carrier becomes unmanageable when used in a cross–country situa-

This photo shows my honker decoys at Modoc National Wildlife Refuge. I found that a dozen of these was enough.

tion. If a carrier is used, the hunter should know his destination before starting out.

I prefer to stick with the backpack as a method for carrying decoys. A good backpack makes carrying decoys quite comfortable and allows the hunter maximum flexibility in terms of the terrain that can be covered. Many decoy bags have straps so that they can be carried like a backpack. I have used some of these, and, in general, they work fine for short distances, but for long trips they are awkward and tend to cause considerable pain. The decoy bags that I've used weren't very durable either. If a strap breaks in the field, the trip home becomes a nightmare. Any external frame backpack will work fine for carrying decoys, the larger the frame the better. The pack itself should be as large as possible. Small compartments is not what's needed for carrying decoys. I have four nylon lashing straps on my pack which allow me to lash on additional bags. Large nylon bags which were originally designed as ball bags have worked well. Other times I've used gunnysacks for additional carrying bags, but they're smaller than the ball bags.

I've seen some custom–made decoy–carrying jackets that appeared to work quite well for carrying about two dozen decoys. I ran into one hunter at Volta Wildlife Area who had built an axle and bicycle wheel arrangement which carried his john boat and decoys. This arrangement appeared to work well and allowed the hunter to use the boat to keep his dog dry when hunting where there was no dry ground. Some decoy carriers can be converted into blinds after the pond is reached. Others float and can be pulled right out into the pond with the decoys inside. This feature makes loading and unloading easier.

How many decoys is enough?

In general I've found that about two dozen good decoys is enough. The biggest exception to that rule came on a day when my good friend Ralph Laughlin and I hunted at Los Banos on a pond that should have been a good spot. All morning long the birds flew over the pond where we sat and then dive-bombed into the next pond. When finished, we walked past the other pond and talked with the hunters. They had fifteen dozen decoys out compared to our three dozen. Apparently, this large of a spread can have a tremendous effect on the ducks. I think that large numbers of decoys have an even greater impact late in the season as ducks become accustomed to holding in large "safe" zones with large concentrations of ducks. In order to experiment with larger numbers of decoys, I plan on buying a decoy carrier before next season. The trade-off will be a loss of flexibility in site selection.

Which species should decoys imitate?

The species of the decoy does have an effect. On a trip to our regular club this year, my brother took notice of a hen sprig that hovered over the only sprig decoy that we had out. We were still putting out decoys at the time. The sprig paid little attention to Rob who was standing only a few yards away. While hovering, the bird quacked softly at the sprig decoy. If there is a choice of species of decoy, then you may want to take the species that you expect to shoot or prefer to shoot. I choose to take a combination of mallard and sprig decoys as one never really knows what type of birds will dominate the action on any given day, or for that matter, during any portion of a particular day. I recently heard prominent guide, Billy Gianquinto, recommend making all your decoys drakes. That makes a lot of sense, especially for sprig where the drakes stand out so clearly.

Equipment

The conditions met on an ordinary duck hunt are a trying test for equipment. High quality equipment, using the best technology available, will increase your enjoyment of duck hunting. Good equipment makes for trouble-free hunting with maximum opportunity for success. What follows is an item-by-item discussion of the equipment that I carry, and some that I don't. Each item will be needed at some time during the course of a season's hunting.

RAIN GEAR: A rain coat is a must for duck hunting. The coat should be camouflaged and not too bulky. It should have a hood and pocket space to carry items that have to be easily reached. A coat with Goretex exterior is the best available. When wearing a Goretex coat and the appropriate amount of clothing, the hunter can stay warm and dry under almost any conditions. I prefer the unlined Goretex coat made by Columbia. The amount of insulation underneath is varied continuously during the course of the hunt. Clothing is removed to prevent sweating while walking or picking up decoys and then added while hunting when the lack of movement makes the cold more noticeable.

COTTON CAMO JACKET: I use cotton clothing during the early season when the weather is warm and dry. I don't leave my Goretex coat at home though.

CAMO HAT: A good hat is a must. It will be the most visible part of the hunter. Goretex is a good material, but there are other materials that work well. The hat

This photo shows my backpack, loaded for a hunt at Modoc National Wildlife Refuge. There are a dozen honker shell decoys in the pack and ten mallard decoys inside the bag. There's room on top for one more decoy bag, if needed.

should have a medium brim that will hide the hunter's face, but not block too much vision. Ear protection from cold is a plus.

TROUSERS: In cold weather, wool trousers are great, but in warm weather cotton is better.

SHIRT: I wear wool, except during early season. Wool will retain its insulating qualities even when wet.

WOOL SWEATER: This is quite effective as a layer that will keep you warm even when wet.

POLYPROPYLENE UNDERWEAR: Polypro wicks moisture away from the body. When your body stays dry it also stays warmer. When polypropylene is combined with wool and Goretex, the hunter's capability to withstand cold and rain is almost unlimited in California hunting situations.

HIKING BOOTS: Many times it's easier and quicker to hike in boots and then put waders on after reaching the pond. This also reduces wear and tear on waders.

WOOL SOCKS AND GLOVES: Once again the capability of wool to insulate when wet is the reason for the selection. I prefer gloves without fingers until the temp drops too low, then I add another pair with fingers.

SCARF: Comes in handy for cleaning glasses and miscellaneous items.

HEADLAMP: Extremely convenient when loading up or travelling in the dark. Leaves your hands available for other important uses.

FLASHLIGHT: Having a light is usually important enough to warrant carrying a spare in case the headlamp fails. Remember to occasionally check the spare light so that it will work when called upon. Ray Burmaster suggests that a piece of string be tied to the hole at the end of a minimag flashlight so that it can be carried around the neck while walking or putting out decoys, this leaves your hands free.

GUN: I'm not an expert on guns. I carry a Winchester model twelve that was given to me as a boy. Important considerations are: being familiar with your gun, having a reliable gun, and being able to hit the birds. Double barrels, pumps and automatics all have their advantages.

SHELLS: I generally use two and three-quarter inch magnum loads, but standard loads are fine over decoys. With the implementation of "steel shot only" regulations, there will be mass confusion among hunters who have not used it before. There is much literature available on the difference between lead and steel, but only field testing will make individual hunters competent with steel shot. It's like learning to shoot ducks all over again. The time will come when steel shot will be accepted and considered an adequate replacement for lead. I have to reduce my ranges when using steel. At close range (inside 35 yards) steel is deadly. At one point in 1986, while using steel shot, I killed 16 birds in a row without losing or crippling any. Lead could have done no better. Judging from my experience, I'll be using #2 shot on ducks. For geese, I'll probably use the largest shot that's made available.

DECOYS: I prefer to carry good–looking decoys, and if necessary, sacrifice numbers for quality. The inflatable decoys that I carry are excellent. Floating goose decoys are an option that I like. Only a couple can be carried on a backpack. With a decoy carrier, I've seen hunters carry a dozen floating goose decoys along with duck decoys. Goose shell–decoys are needed for honker hunting and I had good success with just a dozen of these. Plastic bags, paper plates, and diapers work well for snow geese. These "garbage" type decoys are cheap and easy to carry. Numbers is the key when using them. Many times my brother and I have put out over 500 paper plates and plastic bags. They tend to work better in cloudy or foggy weather. The sun glistens off the plastic on clear days and the bags become transparent. Obviously its important (and also hard work) to pick up all of these decoys when the hunt is over, so be sure to give this (clean up) consideration before you start.

DECOY CARRIER: If you intend to carry more than about three dozen decoys by yourself, you'll need a carrier. There are several on the market. Some of the best are home made.

BACKPACK: Any sturdy external frame pack will do. Lashing straps make adding decoy bags easier.

EAR PLUGS: I consider these to be a must. I use the sonic earplugs that let you hear somewhat. Each hunter has a different susceptibility to ear damage, but no one should hunt without ear protection.

DUCK CALL: I carry an Iverson mallard call, a Four–In–One whistle and a wooden whistle.

GOOSE CALLS: Snow goose, honker and spec calls. I like the OLT honker and specklebelly calls. Most snow goose calls work fine.

COMPASS: This is a needed item on foggy days in unknown areas. I left mine behind one trip this year and was quite limited by thick fog.

MAP: All refuges provide maps that are generally indispensable. The start and stop times are on the back of the map, as well as other important refuge information.

DUCK STRAP: Get one with a wide shoulder strap.

EXTRA NYLON CORD: Comes in handy for tying things on pack, making repairs, or carrying ducks.

WATER BOTTLE: Your body needs water even on cold days.

INSPECT REPELLANT: Especially needed in the early season.

CAMERA: In addition to photographing your trophies, you will find interesting wildlife photo opportunities on the refuges.

MASK OR FACE PAINT: The face is the first thing that the birds spot . Face camo is more important when hunting from a natural blind than it is when hunting out of a permanent blind.

WATCH: Important at all refuges if you want to get in all of your allowed hunting time without risk of citation. The watch is even more important at Merced, Tulelake, or Lower Klamath where the closing times are at mid-day.

SUN GLASSES: On sunny days they will save your eyes and make duck identification easier.

FIELD GLASSES: Nice to have when searching for a new spot. You'll be able to see birds working that might otherwise go unnoticed. Sometimes they will allow you to spot a hunter who is already in the spot that you're heading for, thus saving you some trouble.

WADERS: Chest-high rubber waders are probably best. LaCross was mentioned by several people as a good brand; Bill Fischer likes Seal Drys. Some hunters use the neoprene waders. Since they are probably too warm for early season, you'll need two pair of waders if you choose neoprene. I was told by one hunter that his neoprene waders were almost two years old and still going strong. He said that he'd done a great deal of hiking in them. Another hunter told me that they're not warm enough in harsh weather. A wader belt and good suspenders are important. They'll keep some of the water out if you fall. For several years I wore waders with no suspenders, and it seemed as if a belt alone was adequate support. Then I realized that the life of my waders was greatly reduced, as holes formed at the knees where they rubbed together. Now I wear suspenders and a belt. Keeping your suspenders tight while walking and then loosening them while hunting will also help reduce wear around the knees. Another trick is to pull inner tube pieces up your legs over the top of your waders. If you get the right size to insure that they'll stay in place, the inner tube will protect the knee area. One of my hunting partners, Fred Hilke, recommends that waders be tested in a swimming pool before the first hunt of each season. This can prevent finding a catastrophic leak after it's too late to do anything about it. (Other than getting wet or going home.)

AMMO BELT: I don't have one of these, but having a belt with 25 shell slots might prevent you from getting zapped for having too many shells by accident. If you carry the weight on your hips, it will be easier on your back.

STOOL: I use a five gallon paint bucket for a stool. Dennis Ludington likes to use a "tule stool" which he makes out of aluminum tubing and diamond plate. There's an adjustable cross bar to keep it from sinking out of sight in the mud.

FIELD GUIDE TO BIRDS: Golden, Peterson's, and the Audubon Society put out field guides that are have good identification information and photos or sketches of all the ducks as well as other marsh birds.

Vehicles

There are several factors that must be considered when choosing a vehicle for refuge duck hunting. Probably the most important consideration is having the ability to sleep comfortably during the night before the hunt. For this reason a camper or recreational vehicle is best. A travel–trailer is sometimes acceptable, but may be excluded due to limitations on parking lot capacity. (I'd like to see travel–trailers allowed at all refuges.) The camper is the best solution. Four–wheel drive is not necessary, but could be useful during the unusual situations that could arise during times of very stormy weather. Any type of vehicle will do if you don't have a choice. The roads on all of the refuges are well maintained.

A travel trailer is convenient and comfortable, but check to make sure that it is permitted at the refuge you choose to hunt.

Experiences In The Field During The 1986/87 Duck Season

Opening Day At Gray Lodge

One would suspect that arriving three days before the start of duck season would be early enough to assure entrance to Gray Lodge Wildlife Area for the start of the season. How many people would come and wait in line for three days in order to hunt on opening morning? The answer became clear as I entered the parking lot on Wednesday, about 7:00 p.m. There were forty or fifty cars parked in a single line. Not knowing where to start, I stopped and spoke to a man who was parked by himself on my right. "What's the situation with the line?" I asked. "I'm in the reservation line and that's the non-reservation line over there," he replied. The other line of cars proved to have fifty-three hunters in it and I took my place as number fifty-four. Discussions with other hunters in line led me to believe that if similar numbers of hunters turned out this year as had turned out in the past, I'd get in on opening morning.

During the following two days, the topic of most discussions was duck hunting. I found that most of the hunters I spoke with considered Gray Lodge to be a very special refuge. Most had hunted this refuge for years and considered themselves to be part of an elite group, a kind of duck hunting fraternity. These were the hard core of Gray Lodge hunters and they treated the waiting period as a warm-up ceremony. Although I told almost all who I talked with that I'd never hunted the refuge before, none gave me even an inkling of specific information about where to hunt. I didn't seek advice, but was surprised that at least some information about the

41

Gray Lodge hunters gather around the picking table, 1976. Photo courtesy of John Cowan.

refuge wasn't volunteered. Apparently, a high value was placed on this information.

The first hunters in line had arrived on Saturday, one full week prior to opening day. Obviously there was more to this for some people that just a duck hunt. One gentleman in line was over seventy years old and had hunted Gray Lodge with his brother almost every opening day for about twenty-five years. The people I met were from many different lines of work– pilots, students, retired military, unemployed, fathers, sons, wives, girlfriends, and brothers. On Thursday night the regulars threw a party and expected nothing in return except that you have a good time. A giant banner flew over the picnic area that read: "GRAND OPENING." John Cowan, a wildlife biologist who is retired from the California Department of Fish and Game, was the guest of honor. For many years, he had been the Gray Lodge manager, and it was obvious that he had won the respect of the hunters there.

As Saturday approached, the number of hunters in the lot grew until it was nearly full. Out of a possible 200 reservations that were issued, 188 showed by Saturday morning; they took 333 of the 400 openings for the refuge. I was in. The last "sweat line" hunter to get in (by shooting time) had probably arrived sometime Thursday morning. Hunters that were too late to get in before shoot time were able to take the place of departing hunters.

The hunting area at Gray Lodge is divided into two zones. The West zone is generally considered to be the best. The closed zone is on the west side of the area and the ducks naturally move towards that zone. By the time I was allowed to enter the refuge, the west side was full and I went to parking lot number six on the east side.

I had spent a great deal of time wondering about this moment. Now was the time for action. What should a hunter do when faced with the problem of hunting an unknown area? Parking lot six was the first lot. I had already decided that this was a good possibility. I figured that many of the hunters would pass up the first lot in order to see what else was available. There were only a few cars in the lot, so I decided to park. Heading south from the lot, I walked along a levee between tule filled ponds which appeared to be in excellent shape. Voices could be heard to the west and they were acting pretty excited about the hunt. I wanted to hunt on my own as much as possible, and I feared that the adreneline in these guys was running too high. I reversed my course and headed north. After passing the parking lot heading in the opposite direction, I came to an area that appeared to have enough open water and no other hunters nearby. It was just about shooting time, so the decision was made. The decoys would go out here.

I wanted to shoot mallards or sprig. Three dozen decoys were placed randomly to the east of me. There was a good place to hide on the edge of the pond. As the sky grew light, ducks began to pass. At shooting time shots rang out in all directions. As the ducks flew by, I realized that while looking into the sunrise, it would be difficult to pick out the mallards and sprig that I had hoped for, especially the drakes. I watched duck after duck go over. Spoonbill, teal, widgeon, teal, widgeon, spoonbill – teal, teal, teal – spoonbill, spoonbill. There were plenty of ducks, but very few of the ones that I was waiting for. At 8:00 a.m. I fired my first shot of the day and killed a hen sprig. I felt a sense of frustration for shooting the hen, but was happy to break the ice. Looking into the sun, I hadn't been able to tell the sex of the duck and had taken a chance. The sun rose higher and the shooting continued. The ducks flew a little faster. A few big ducks came over, but only the teal, widgeon, and spoonbill wanted to work my decoys. The decision was made to move out into the pond and kneel down in a small clump of grass where the birds would be closer to me. I knelt there until my knees ached badly. Ducks continued to work the decoys, many teal and some others that I couldn't identify. I could hold out a while longer. When I finally did stand up, the pain in my knees was so bad that I had to stand there for a couple of minutes and limber up my legs.

When I got back to the levee, I sat down for a break and a cart wheel squeaked as a hunter came down the road towards me. Somebody had their ducks and was heading in. As the hunters passed, I checked their ducks. They had all greenheads and drake sprig, two beautiful limits of ducks. Obviously, there were better spots than mine.

The next decision was easy; I picked up my decoys and headed north along the levee in the direction from which the cart had come. The ponds opened up and became large, open ponds, the type that mallards and sprig like. I could see now what my problem had been. The first pond selected had been far too small. I found a patch of tules to hide in and threw the decoys out in all directions, anxious to recommence the hunt. As I got set up, a hunter to the north of me searched for a downed duck. I decided to help him as other ducks probably wouldn't work until he got back into his blind anyway. I hoped that my dog "Tubbs" would find the bird in the thick grass, but it was eventually given up for lost. We headed back to hide and wait for ducks. It was now about 9:00 a.m. I called and ducks worked, but no big ducks came within range. The hunters to the north of me were doing a lot of shooting and within an hour or so they hollered over that they were heading in and that maybe I should try their spot as the ducks seemed to like it. I took up their offer and moved my decoys for the second time.

This new location was duck utopia. This must have been the spot where the earlier limits of mallard and sprig had come from. The ducks loved it. It was the northeast corner of a large pond and the prevailing wind was out of the north, so it allowed the ducks to come down while over open water. There was a nice patch of dry brush to hide in and about the only thing wrong with the blind location was that the hunter had to look right into the bright sun, and I hadn't brought my sunglasses with me.

It was 10:30 a.m. when I got set up for the third and final time. I knew that I was now in the best possible spot and no further moving would be necessary. It was clear and hot. There were still plenty of ducks working the area as I hid in the blind holding out for mallards and sprig. Although it wasn't required at Gray Lodge, I was shooting steel shot. This was to be my first experience with the unpopular shells. I didn't really know what to expect from the loads when a greenhead came in fast from the north with the wind. He was so close that I couldn't resist the temptation to shoot the down-wind shot. Boom-miss, Boom-miss –no he was hit –and going down. He hit the water about a quarter mile away and I took off after him. Approaching the spot where he had gone down, a greenhead took off out of range and after finding nothing else in the area, I decided that this must have been the bird I was after. I headed back to the blind, disappointed.

Spoonbill and widgeon worked the pond constantly and there was a temptation to give up on my goal of mallards and sprig, but I held steadfast. Another greenhead came in over

45

the decoys, boom–miss, boom–miss. At least it was a clean miss. I held on and waited as the less desirable ducks continued to work the decoys. Other hunters could see the birds working and started to move in on the area, probably wondering why I wasn't shooting. It would be tougher now as a group of four hunters set up downwind of me about 250 yards away. Any ducks heading for me had to pass over them first. A greenhead made it through the maze of hunters and I hit him with the first shot, but he recovered and didn't go down. Now I was feeling bad. It was about noon and I was wasting too many opportunities. The number of mallards and sprig were constantly getting thinner, but the spoonies and widgeon seemed to be endless. A drake sprig passed over in range and I fired. Boom, no dice. A short while later another drake came over, gliding into the wind. Boom–miss, boom-hit, but he managed to glide for about a mile before I lost sight of him going down to the east. I blamed the steel shot. It was now about 3:00 p.m.. I had blown chances on enough mallards and sprig to fill my limit. My eyes ached from staring into the sun. I was drenched in sweat from the sun beating on my waders. The decision was made to shoot at spoonies and end my miseries.

The first spoony came in with the wind and at twenty–five yards I fired. Boom–miss, boom–miss. Maybe this wouldn't be as easy as I thought! Another spoony came in and he went down with two shots. Then another with the same result. Five more shots at three spoonies and I had my limit and headed in.

Comments

At the start of this hunt I began to formulate ideas for techniques that could be used to increase success when hunting in unknown territory. My ideas had been mostly ineffective. I would have done best by waiting and watching for a period of time until a good location could be found. I travelled only a short distance from the car and that was a disadvantage. When I set up, I should have taken the rising sun into consideration. It is possible to scout an area prior to opening day. To do this you must go to the refuge about two weeks in advance. Call ahead to verify when the area gets closed off. By scouting the area in advance, a couple of good locations can be identified and then secured in the dark, ahead of competition.

I used steel shot for the first time on this hunt. I used #4 shot and since have decided that #4 is too small for mallards and sprig. The reason that I crippled so many birds was the small shot size and lack of experience with shooting steel.

Volta Teal

It was about 2:00 a.m. when my brother, Rob, and I drove east on Interstate 580 towards the San Joaquin Valley where we would turn south on Interstate 5 towards Volta Wildlife Area. The drive would take approximately one-and-a-half hours. Rob hadn't bought a duck stamp yet, but had decided to go along for the outing. Reports about Volta had been good, as hunters had averaged about four ducks per gun on opening weekend, predominately teal.

While I was at Gray Lodge a hunter had recommended that I try Pond Ten at Volta, so I decided to take his advice. It was about a mile from parking lot two to the northeast corner of the refuge. The hike was easy. We walked straight down a levee along the large canal that runs through the center of the refuge. After the levee took a slow 90 degree turn to the right, we then took a sharp 90 degree turn to the left and found a medium sized pond with tules on its north side and sagebrush on its south side. In the darkness it appeared to be an excellent spot. Rob helped me put about two dozen decoys out near the center of the pond, and I knelt down next to a clump of sagebrush as shooting time arrived.

There were plenty of ducks. I could have started shooting right away, but decided to wait to see if there would be many of the larger ducks working the pond. Teal came in readily and several landed in my decoys. A few mallards and sprig were in the area, but they tended to stay high over the pond where we hid. They often came down to the north, over tules and hunters in that area knocked down several of them.

After about a half hour of waiting without firing a shot, it was time to start shooting since this activity possibly wouldn't continue. Teal passed over my decoys continuously. Several times, I almost took marginal shots before I realized that the decoys were too far from the blind. Rob helped me rearrange them closer to the sagebrush blind, and then I was in business. The teal continued to come in directly over the decoys. I took nothing but easy thirty yard shots and still managed to miss a couple of ducks. By 9:00 a.m. I had five green wing teal, and it was time to head into town for breakfast.

Rob had also noticed that the pond to the north had done well for big ducks. I had an urge to return and hunt that spot on another trip. It had been a fun and relaxing morning, and it had also been good shooting. The five teal were killed with eight shots. This was the best I'd ever done. Maybe it was possible to kill five ducks with five shots.

Comments

For the first time in an area, this was an unusually successful hunt. The information that a Gray Lodge hunter had given to me about Pond Ten had been quite beneficial. In general, directions to a particular area at a refuge must be accepted carefully. I found that hunters tended to give out better information about other refuges than the one being currently hunted. Sometimes, I traded information with other hunters. By trading information, both parties can benefit from an exchange. When following another hunter's directions into the field, one must use extreme caution. Many times hunters think they remember the directions to a good spot, but forget about one turn, which can create a serious problem. In the dark, you are at the mercy of the one who gave you directions.

A good portion of a morning can be wasted by following incorrect directions.

Afternoon Success At Volta

When I got out of bed on Saturday morning, I thought about hunting ducks. I had the urge to go back to Volta and try for the pond that had looked so good on Wednesday. Maybe the solution would be to arrive late and try an afternoon shoot. Hunting in the afternoon might be the best chance that I'd have for getting that popular and apparently productive location. I got to the pond about 11:00 a.m. and as expected, there were decoys out. The hunters there were getting some shooting. There was a place for me to hunt on the far side of the pond. When they left, I could pick up my decoys and move.

I found a location on a large canal that seemed to be reasonable. Hiding there in the tules, I watched for ducks. Judging from the activity around the decoys, one would think that there wasn't a duck on the entire refuge, but, to the southeast of me the hunters on the good pond were getting continuous action. Every few minutes one or two ducks would show up and drop straight down to the pond they liked. I hoped that the hunters there would be finished early.

At 1:00 p.m. I heard the sound of decoys banging against each other as they do when hunters pick them up. I got excited and rushed to collect my decoys which were now spread all over the area. When I got to the desired pond, it was vacant and I quickly put out nine mallard decoys and left the rest in my pack. If needed, they could be put out later. I had just settled in when two other hunters appeared who had designs on the spot. They settled for a different location, about 200 yards away. I wanted to try for sprig and mallards so the spoonbills and widgeon were passed up and several landed in my decoys. Some flew within range of the other hunters and they shot at them. I blew on my mallard call and sprig whistle. A short whistle every couple seconds worked well and a group of about ten sprig came in overhead about twenty yards high with their wings set. As they came out of the sun I pulled up and fired. Boom–hit. Boom–hit. A double on drake sprig. Now this was the ticket! I had waded out into the pond to retrieve the ducks before I realized that the second bird was a widgeon. The chance for the perfect limit was ruined already. No big deal. I still hadn't missed, and this was a great opportunity for the five shot limit.

I hid in the tule island which was located in the center of the pond and called. A stiff breeze picked up, and the ducks came in continuously. Some spoonbills landed, but I waited. A group of mallards came in as I called. They circled the blind once. Then they passed with their wings set. They were about ten yards off the water and thirty yards from me when I pulled up and dropped a drake. Now the goal was within reach. I waited patiently. A drake sprig came out of the east. He was low enough but was flying fast and wasn't interested in the decoys. There wasn't much time to decide. He was directly over me as I fired. The opportunity was too good to pass up. Boom. He kept on flying. I fired again. Boom. His wing beat slowed. He kept on going, gradually sinking. Determined not to loose sight of him I stretched up to see over the tules and took a step to the right while watching the duck fade in the west. My feet went out from under me and I fell into the water on my back. The only thing on my mind was to keep the bird in sight, so I climbed to my feet and spotted him again. Another step to the right; I lost my footing again and fell into the two–foot deep water, face first. I swam. After staggering to my feet, I almost sprinted across the pond. It was important to get to the bird quickly. If he were alive, he would swim into the tules and escape. I was drenched, but the bird was found on the water about 300 yards from the blind. One bird to go and even though it wouldn't be a five–shot limit, it was still a chance to get every bird shot at and a very respectable limit of ducks.

Some time passed and the other hunters nearby continued to shoot an occasional spoony, but most of the ducks liked the pond where I hid, and birds continued to land around me. I called and waited. Finally three drake mallards came in close. I called and waited. I tried to get them to pass over the tules. They took note of the calling and circled the blind at forty yards. I wanted a sure shot. After the third pass they drifted down into the decoys and landed only thirty-five yards away. They couldn't be allowed to get away with this, so I stepped from the tules. As they lifted off, I picked out the closest drake and fired. Boom. He kept going. Boom. No noticeable result. Boom. I fired one more time. The rate of his wing beat slowed. He made it to the edge of the pond, where he hit the water and quit moving. I had my ducks, and had shot at only five.

Comments

The key to success here was getting the right spot, and then waiting for the nearly point-blank shot. If you get a spot that is this good, then be selective and you'll increase your success. In order to shoot all big ducks, one must be willing to kill a few less ducks at times. Often, big ducks won't come in until they see the other ducks working the area. The widgeon, teal and spoonbill become decoys that encourage the mallards and sprig to come in. If the smaller ducks are shot at, you'll never know what may have been.

Colusa Marsh

On November twenty-sixth, the day before Thanksgiving, I rose about 3:00 a.m., made my now routine stop at a Seven-Eleven near home, and got out of town at 3:45 a.m. Traveling north on Interstate 5, I knew the trip from Livermore to Colusa National Wildlife Refuge would take between two-and-a-half to three hours. Fog slowed travel, but would provide weather suitable for duck hunting. This was a welcome change from the clear, warm weather of late.

Colusa is a relatively small refuge when compared to Sacramento and Delevan refuges which are nearby. Of the approximately 4000 acres which make up the refuge about 1200 are huntable. I looked at my topography map of the area and decided to hunt the west side of the refuge. (I tried using topo maps to study the refuge layouts before each hunt. I found them to be of little value.)

I headed west, looking for a pond that turned out to be part of a tule marsh. It was already shooting time as I walked along a levee on the north edge of the refuge. There was no shooting and a drake mallard flew low over the tules, a good sign. To my amazement, there were no hunters on the pond that I had selected and none nearby. All indications suggested that I was on my own in this area of the refuge. Through the fog, which permitted about 100 yards visibility, I could see a red-tailed hawk resting undisturbed. Many birds were swimming in or standing around the pond as I entered the water. There were several great blue herons and great egrets in the area. In the fog most of the animals didn't appear to notice my presence. I decided to place my newly acquired snow goose decoys in the center of the pond and hide in the tules to the south of them. It would be best to wait for more clues about how the ducks worked before putting out the rest of my modest spread, which was about ten decoys. A pair of mallards swam out of the tules in the exact spot where I was about to hide. They took off and disappeared into the fog. I hadn't even thought about loading my gun yet. It was encouraging to see ducks using the area.

Standing in the tules, the stillness of the marsh was impressive and Interstate 5 could be vaguely heard in the distance to the west. Marsh sounds periodically broke the silence. The groawk ... groawk of a great blue heron could be heard from nearby tules. I tried my mallard call, but it seemed too loud. Two teal came straight out of the fog and passed on the left. Before a move could be made to shoot, they disappeared back into the fog. Calling wouldn't bring them back. A short while later, two mallards passed over the snow goose decoys about twenty-five yards high. I called and they made a sweeping turn passing directly overhead, an easy shot. I responded by missing them twice. The ducks were close enough, so I contributed the miss to an inability to turn and shoot in the thick mud of the marsh. (At the time I didn't stop to wonder if these were the same two mallards that I'd flushed a few minutes earlier. Later in the season, after having flushed ducks return on several occasions, I decided that ducks will often return to the pond from which they were disturbed. I'm pretty sure that a hunting strategy could be formed from this situation, where jumped ducks are not shot at. The hunter should then hide and wait for about fifteen minutes. Often as not, the ducks will return to see if the danger has passed.)

Despite the miss, my attitude was good. Two ducks came in from the right. They passed by very close with cupped wings. The air passing over their wings made a loud sound. They were probably mallards. The incredible speed with which they passed made it almost impossible to shoot. The noise seemed to be caused by efforts to brake their speed. They landed about seventy-five yards to the west. At this time it didn't seem that it was important to shoot "all the shots" anyway. After the ducks landed, one of them started to call in a very regular pattern of highballs and single quacks. The live duck provided a great example to pattern calling after.

Two widgeon or gadwall passed over the decoys just out of range. Off to my right a duck was coming in. It came into view at a range of about 300 yards. It was heading straight at me with cupped wings and moving very fast, just as the two previous ducks had done. Once again the identity of the duck was unclear. When he got directly overhead, I shot. Broken wing. Shot again. Missed. He hit the water off to my left where the other ducks had landed. I found the duck and retrieved it after shooting it twice on the water. It was a gadwall. That's what the other ducks were too. While chasing the duck, several others took off from the same area. Apparently, this was the spot that they liked, so I spread my mallard decoys out in the general vicinity. The ducks were placed in groups of twos and threes, scattered as the live ducks had been. This was in contrast to my usual method of clumping them all together. I brought my bucket out to sit on and hid deep in the tules about thirty yards from the bulk of the decoys.

Marsh wrens climbed in the tules only a few feet away. They are one of my favorite birds with very delicate and beautiful markings. The duck hunting slowed down, but this was definitely a good location. A flock of curlews flew over and harriers were busy hunting in the marsh. Two different types of sandpipers walked in the shallow water along the shore. Black shouldered kites and red-tailed hawks were observed working the fields to the west. A flock of snowy egrets passed over. This marsh was densely inhabited. Several groups of widgeon and gadwall worked the decoys, but I decided to hold off for a while and hope for mallards or sprig, but none came. Some of the ducks landed in the decoys, but I continued to hold out for mallards. About mid-day I decided to end my holdout and shoot at any available ducks. My second duck decoyed in to about twenty yards and was hit on the second shot. Another gadwall. Two teal passed on the left; two more misses. Eleven shots and only two ducks. Not too impressive. I swore at the steel shot. That was obviously the problem, but unfortunately for me the worst was yet to come. I took nothing but close shots; most within thirty yards. The more I missed, the closer I let them come and the worse my shooting became.

I decided to take a short walk. I'm not much for jump-shooting, but a change of pace was in order. Two wood ducks sprang from the water twenty-five yards away, an easy shot – boom...miss, boom...miss, boom...miss. Frustration! A few minutes later a teal – boom...miss, boom...miss. Now I was fit to be tied. Nine shots left; there was still a chance to save face. I headed back to my decoys.

A group of hunters passed by about 300 yards to the south. They were making quite a racket and also getting some shooting. Fortunately for me they didn't stay in the area long. Soon the birds started to work again. Two teal passed by on the edge of range, but they weren't close enough. This situation called for the best chance possible. They landed near the goose decoys along with a small group of widgeon. Four more ducks worked around almost in range. Four mallards came in from the west. When shots were fired to the south, they all departed. It was now about 3:30.

After a few minutes, two gadwall worked in over the tules. I called and they did a nose–dive right at me. At twenty yards I pulled up; boom...miss, boom...miss, boom... finally a hit and another gadwall. This was becoming a record day...for missed shots! I had recorded eleven straight misses; what a drought. With six shots left, there was still a reasonable chance for a five–duck limit. I waited for a good shot. Two more gadwall appeared. I called, and they came right in. Boom...miss, boom...miss, boom...miss. How could I miss? Three shots were left. Disgusted with my shooting; I quit worrying about a limit and decided to get it over with by shooting the last three shots at the next available duck. It didn't take long. Two ducks came in from the left. They passed at twenty–five yards; widgeon. Boom....miss. Boom....miss. Boom....miss.... No, ...wait. He wavered, shuddered, and dropped. One hundred yards away he lay on the pond. I forgot my frustration and strode for the duck as if it were a drake mallard. My poor shooting was forgotten. At least I'd ended on a good note. It had been a good day. I'd seen plenty of wildlife, and had had more than enough chances to get my ducks.

Comments

I did just about everything right on this hunt, except shoot straight. After learning more about shooting steel shot, I would have gone home early on a day like this. The ingredients of success here were foggy weather, an isolated spot, and locating the exact spot where the ducks wanted to land. The day before Thanksgiving is probably a good day to remember as a low attendance day. Other similar days are Christmas Eve and New Year's Eve if they fall on shoot days as they did in 1986.

Tule Lake Spaced Blinds

On December ninth, I decided to hunt the spaced blinds at Tule Lake National Wildlife Refuge. The spaced blinds are nothing more than stakes driven into the ground at intervals providing marked locations for hunters to hunt from. This process guarantees hunters a reasonable distance between themselves and other hunters. The hunters that show up at the check station before 5:30 a.m. are included in a drawing for spaces. The refuge manager in charge selects the blinds that he feels will be the best and includes enough of them in the drawing for everybody present to get one. Each group of hunters has an equal chance for the blinds that have been most successful. If a hunter wants a certain blind to be included in the drawing, he can ask that it be included. If a hunter shows up after the drawing, he can choose a blind from those that remain.

Due to an alarm clock malfunction, I arrived after the drawing and chose a blind from out of the remainders. I didn't feel disadvantaged by the late selection and was optimistic as I ventured out into the fog. It was quite foggy and it was mainly due to the fog that hunters had been successful the day before. The news of the previous day's success had brought the hunters out in force.

At shooting time I had my dozen honker decoys out on one side of me and about twenty plastic bags out on the other. I hid in some tall grass. The field was white as snow from the fog which was frozen onto the grass. Visibility was about 100 yards and I couldn't see any other hunters. Only a few white front geese and cackling geese flew into range and the season for both species was closed, so I waited patiently. A large flock of snow geese could be heard to the southeast of me along with shooting by other hunters. Each time the geese would rise up they would create a tremendous roar. At one point a flock of ross's geese flew by low and just out of range. After four hours of hunting with the feeling that geese were all around me, it was hard to believe that I still hadn't fired a shot.

At 12:15, I unloaded my gun and put the shells neatly back into the box from which they'd come. I closed the lid on the box and looked up. One hundred yards away, and ten yards off the ground, were three honkers. They had their wings set and were gliding directly towards my decoys. I quickly reloaded my gun and looked up as the birds made the last flap of their wings before hitting the ground about sixty yards away. They were between me and the decoys. I debated about what to do. Mentally I was done hunting. Even though my watch said 12:15, I wasn't absolutely sure that the time was correct. The birds were right on the edge of range, but I could probably get at least one of them if I tried. These factors added up to make a situation that I didn't feel comfortable about. I decided to unload my gun and let them live. I'd have to wait for another day to kill a honker.

Comments

If I'd been hiding closer to the decoys, I probably would have been so close to the approaching birds that I wouldn't have passed up the shot. There's the increased chance that they'll see you when setting up close, so you must have a better blind. I'd recommend setting up between twenty-five and forty yards from the decoys. You need to be close to honkers for a sure kill. When they're fooled, as these were, honkers will come right in on the decoys. I saw this again on later hunts at Modoc and Ash Creek.

Although the location which I picked had seemed all right to me, it was obvious that I would have been better off if I had gotten to the drawing to take advantage of the refuge manager's knowledge of the most recent flight patterns. Many of the hunters had success on this day. Next time I'll be more careful about getting to the refuge early. For much of the season, this area has a tremendous concentration of snow geese.

Lower Klamath in December

On December eleventh, I arrived at the entrance to Lower Klamath National Wildlife Refuge at about 5 a.m. The refuge wouldn't be open to the public until 5:30 a.m., so I waited and listened to the news on the radio. The weather was moderate for December in the Klamath Basin, and the word was that the hunting for Canada Geese wouldn't pick up until the weather got colder. As it was, most of the ponds were frozen and there weren't many duck hunters around.

Most of the hunters who were there were concentrating on Area Twelve and I was told that there was at least one group of hunters that had done well on honkers the day before in that area. While driving around the refuge during the afternoon of the previous day, I had seen a flock of honkers feeding in Area Eight. I decided to hunt there as I'd probably be the only hunter in that area, and that's the way that I prefer to hunt.

It was a long walk to the desired location and I didn't get set up until daylight. It was tricky making it to the spot without waders as there was a large canal around the field. I set up my dozen honker shells and waited. Very few geese came within eyesight let alone gun range and by 10:30 a.m., I was ready to try something else.

The Lower Klamath Refuge closes at 1:00 p.m. so I had to hurry if anything of consequence was to be tried. While driving around on Wednesday, I had photographed several groups of spoonbills feeding in small pockets of ice free water. Since many of these birds were in areas that were open to hunting and nobody was hunting in these areas today, I started searching for an appropriate "spoony pocket". Because Area Seven is a closed zone, the parking lot just to the

While driving the refuge in the afternoon, I spotted these Spoonbills feeding through holes the ice.

north of it was a logical place to start. Tubbs and I walked around the area and I couldn't find a spot that looked good except for an area only about 150 yards from the parking lot. Since the water there was too deep for wading, I sat down to see if any ducks would pass overhead.

I was impressed with the number of spoonbills landing in the area, but in water that appeared to be just out of reach. A hunter walked by who I had met the day before and he suggested that I walk along the tules where the ice was thick and hunt the patch right in front of me. When I walked through the tules, I found that the water under the ice wasn't as deep as I had assumed. It was easy to reach the area where the ducks had been landing. Once I discovered this, the rest was easy. I didn't even need decoys. I just called from the tules and waited for the birds to fly out of the closed zone. After they took off, they almost always flew to the same spot.

I used the mallard call and made just enough calls to keep the birds off the water. As they approached they would dip down over the open patch of water and as they prepared to land, I'd call. They frequently flew directly over me about twenty yards high. I missed the first two shots, but after recalling what a friend had told me recently, I started to shoot directly at the birds. (Ron Cole, who is a biologist at Tule Lake, convinced me that the best approach is to shoot directly at the birds. He compares shooting steel to an electronic shooting gallery, where the birds drop as soon as you pull the trigger.) During the next hour, my opinion of steel shot was dramatically changed. Once a feel for the speed of the shot was developed, I found that the birds were easy to hit. This was especially true on close shots. The steel shot was deadly. Only one bird came down alive. I hit five out of the next six birds that I shot at, and have been a firm believer in the effectiveness of steel shot ever since that day.

Comments

The success of this hunt was due to observation, both on the day before the hunt and on the day of the hunt. Many times you won't notice the activity that goes on until you sit down and quietly observe. These birds were landing right next to one of the refuges main roads, but went unnoticed until I started shooting at them. By the time I left, there were about five hunters in the parking lot. They had come to find out what all the shooting was about.

Modoc Honkers

I arrived at Modoc National Wildlife Refuge on Monday, December sixteenth. Modoc is open on different days from other refuges. Tuesday, Thursday, and Saturday are hunt days at Modoc. This is convenient for traveling hunters, who can hunt at Ash Creek or Honey Lake on Sunday and Wednesday. Located right at Alturas, Modoc has excellent access. No overnight camping is allowed and the parking lots are closed prior to one and one-half hours before and one and one-half hours after hunting hours.

Honkers often remain in small family groups like this one, feeding in the closed zone at Modoc NWR.

When asked at a local sporting goods store the merchant told me that the north lot was probably the best spot to start. I stopped at the north lot first, but decided to go for a walk around the southern portion of the refuge, before making a final decision where to actually hunt. I found one spot in the southern area that had some possibilities. A couple teal and later a goldeneye provided chances for shots, but there was no way that my dog would retrieve them through the ice covered water so they were granted a reprieve. I was more interested in finding a spot to hunt for later in the day anyway.

My dog, "Tubbs" ran and had a great time chasing pheasants which were quite numerous as we walked the levees. There were very few hunters on the refuge. Two hunters to the west made a sneak on a pond with a tremendous flock of honkers on it, but their efforts went to waste when the birds got up out of range. Later a friendly hunter warned that great caution should be used when wading the ponds in this area, as some are quite deep.

Satisfied with the general layout of the southern area, I decided to drive to the northern lot and scout it out after breakfast in town. Hunters were more numerous on the northern part of the refuge. From the road several large spreads of giant 747 Canada goose decoys could be seen. They were laid out on a smooth plowed field about forty yards from thick cover where the hunters were hidden from view. Shots had been fired from this area earlier in the day, but there had been no indication of the their degree of success.

After breakfast I walked the mowed marsh grass areas near the north parking lot, where I had seen two honkers landing in the morning. The area that looked most interesting, was covered with goose droppings. I decided to hunt this potentially ideal spot. As two hunters passed me on their way in from hunting, they stated that they had hunted that very spot a few nights back and had been successful. They warned that it would be best toa hunt from a location with no haystacks as the geese were cautious of anything that could conceal a hunter.

An open area with a small patch of grass provided a spot large enough to hide in, but (I hoped) small enough so that the geese wouldn't shy from it. It would be best to place the decoys to the east and thus avoid looking into the setting sun. A few duck decoys fit in nicely on a small patch of frozen irrigation water only a few feet away. When called, Tubbs came over and lay quietly at my feet. Covered almost entirely with hay, we became almost invisible about thirty yards from the goose decoys. It was 2:30. A couple of other hunters came out and set up nearby. While laying there almost perfectly still, the olt honker call was drawn from my jacket and the goose impersonation began. Oonk. Onk. Oonk... Oonk... Oonk... Oonk. Onk...Onk... Oonk... Oonk... Oonk. Off to the east geese could be vaguely heard and this was encouraging. The trick now would be to lay still and stay relaxed. Actually, it was quite comfortable there and sooner than expected the sounds that honkers make when taking to the air could be heard to the east, probably from the closed zone. Oonk. Oonk... Oonk... Oonk... Oonk... onka onka onka onka...

Oonk... Oonk. It seemed incredible, but a large group of honkers were making an enormous racket to the west and it sounded as if they were coming in towards the decoys. It felt like the hair on the back of my neck was stiffening. Oonk. Oonk. Oonk...Oonk... onka onka... onka... onka onka. This was the time to stay motionless and calm. They were definitely bearing down on the decoys. Tubbs snored. Straining to watch for them, I knew that they would pass over any minute. Sure enough there they were sixty yards off to the right. There were about twenty honkers...no more than ten yards off the ground. I felt a hot flash, but didn't move. They were about to land; maybe in range. They glided, almost without motion, turned left about 100 yards out and passed across my toes. Then they turned to the west and landed. They were about seventy-five yards away.

I figured that if I could just lie still, certainly another group of geese would follow them in. What better decoys than twenty live honkers! Not more than thirty seconds went by when a straggler could be heard. He was sounding single honks in a monotonous pattern. Onk...Onk...Onk...Onk. He passed to the right of the decoys just as the others had. This must be it. A strained effort was made to hold back my excitement. He turned left as the others had done. My eyeballs strained. He passed over the other birds. Without slowing, he turned towards the decoys. At full speed he reached the thirty yard range as I saw double. While trying to leap up to shoot, hay went everywhere. The parka hood covered my eyes. A sane man would have just brushed it out of the way, but in my panic, it became a major obstacle. Hood out of the way, I realized that he was too close, but didn't hold my fire. At ten yards the shot would rip large holes in his breast, but that was not to be, as no damage was done with the two point-blank misses. In the panic the second shell case failed to eject cleanly from my model twelve and by the time the third shot was chambered, it became no more than a parting gesture at long range. Shell shocked I stood in disgrace. I'd heard about the hunter that missed honkers that were "unmissable." I never thought it would happen to me.

I tried to be optimistic. A few shots could be heard in nearby fields as more geese made their afternoon feeding flights. Laying back down, it seemed as if there was still an excellent chance. It was still early and geese could be heard calling in several directions. Several groups of geese came in and started to work, but shooting nearby spooked them before they came into range. Off to the right I could hear a hunter blowing on a mallard call. Suddenly a drake sprig appeared out of the corner of my eye, twenty yards off to the right. He turned over the duck decoys about ten feet off the ground. My first inclination was to wait for him to make a second pass. The second thought was that it would be a mistake to wait as he was very close. Coming halfway to my feet, I realized that it was now a marginal shot, and I lay back down. I had blown another opportunity, but it was better to miss an opportunity, than to fire an ill advised shot which would probably scare other birds that might be heading into the area. A single shot from the direction that he'd departed was probably his demise.

Covering up again, I began calling. Once again geese were heard to the west, from my blind side. They were coming in. Passing on the right as the others had done they were close and low. They swung across my toes and turned to their left again giving me the same shot that I had practiced earlier. This time I would not fail. Their honking shifted to a different sound that they sometimes make while landing. When they were at thirty-five yards, I calmly rose to my feet. They flared away, and, at thirty yards, I fired; boom...feathers, boom...he's sinking, boom...he's down. He'd been hit on all three shots, but it wouldn't have been a good idea to take a chance and try for a second bird. Geese will sometimes fall halfway to the ground before regaining their senses and disappearing over the horizon. I was disappointed by the bird's size as it was a lesser Canada goose and not a huge goose as the other had been, but it was a trophy to me none the less.

My efforts to continue the hunt ended when a hunter in the next field crippled a big honker which led Tubbs and I on a chase. It ended when I finished the bird off with a ground shot. Tubbs had chased the bird away from the pursuing hunter and I felt obligated to give him a hand. One honker had made the hunt a success as far as I was concerned, so there was no need to continue hunting this day. As the sun set, the refuge was turned back over to it's rightful owners.

Comments

Observation and discussions with other hunters turned up this spot which was the area with the most activity on the refuge that afternoon. The honkers worked extremely well this day and I didn't hear any reasons being given by the hunters afterward. Many were successful, where few had gotten any chances in the morning. My friend Ron Cole, who frequently hunts honkers in the Klamath Basin, prefers the afternoon shoot. I'd have to agree that it seemed best on this day.

One dozen goose decoys had been plenty; in fact, it could be that, in this situation, a dozen good stand–up type decoys were more realistic to the geese than a large group of decoys would have been. The geese were flying in small family groups so more than a dozen decoys would have been out of the ordinary. This is also a situation where there would have been no advantage or possibly even a disadvantage to having magnum decoys. It's nice to know that sometimes the lighter load will also produce the best results.

The Shutout

Eight times in 1987 I was shutout. Shutouts are common in duck hunting, and the wildlife refuges have bad days just as any duck club does. Four times on these trips, I didn't fire a shot. On most of the shutouts, I had few if any good chances to kill a duck. In six cases out of the eight, I stayed and hunted until the end of shooting time so it's not as if I didn't put forth the effort necessary to kill a duck.

When you hunt a club only, you have the disadvantage of being stuck in one location. Our club in the delta has its up and down days. Above: Rob (my brother), Fred Hilke and I grin after early limits of geese. Below: Rob, Larry DiPietro, Rich Palmer and I grin after a good day of sunshine and fresh air.

Sometimes, there just aren't very many ducks around and no wisdom or effort will change that. Other times there are plenty of ducks, but they are able to spend the periods when hunters are in the field, hiding in safe havens. Closed areas, large bodies of open water, and non-hunted private property, provide such opportunities for evasion.

Most often it's the weather that creates the type of day when no ducks will be killed. On six of the eight days that I was "skunked," the weather was clear and the ducks and geese could see for miles in all directions. Clear weather doesn't guarantee failure, but it certainly reduces the chance for success, especially if there is no wind or cold. When the weather is clear, ducks and geese can spot large concentrations of birds in safe areas. When they see other ducks, they will cover long distances at high altitude and not come down into shooting range until they are over the safe area. When the shooting starts, the ducks will head for these areas and not come back until after the shooting stops.

Obviously, I don't have a solution to that type of day. If I did, I wouldn't have gone home "duckless" so many times in 1986/87. The number one factor controlled by the hunter which can reduce the chance of being stopped cold, is knowledge of an area. In all refuges there are spots that will provide opportunities to shoot ducks on the slow days. Knowledge of a refuge not only means knowing the spots where the ducks are, but also checking to find out how many hunters are in various parts of the refuge on that particular day. Experience is the key to success in this situation. Also, some other tactics may work: jump shooting, walking to remote areas of the refuge, making sure that no early morning opportunities are missed, pass shooting along the edge of closed zones, and watching with field glasses to spot groups of birds landing in areas where hunters have departed.

I enjoy bird watching, and on slow duck hunting days there are always many opportunities to spot interesting birds. Harriers, red-tailed hawks, black shouldered kites and rough-legged hawks are almost always available for observation and are quite fascinating. Small birds are among the most challenging to identify and will approach the well concealed hunter quite closely. Multitudes of shorebirds live in the refuges and one can spend enjoyable hours identifying them. Many of the attractions provided in duck hunting can also be obtained by bird watching. One of my favorite birds is the tiny march wren that is found on every refuge. I sometimes carry my camera and try to photograph the birds of the marsh. Learning to recognize the various species of birds has been quite rewarding to me, and plenty of new discoveries are always being made.

Sometimes these clear "duckless" days are a good time to go walking and look for new places to hunt. I enjoy taking just a couple of mallard decoys and searching the edges of the refuge for pockets where birds may gather in the afternoon. Tossing two mallard decoys into a remote pond and calling from a tule patch can bring in a couple birds. It's pretty unlikely that much action will be drummed up this way, but a little action is better than an early trip home as far as I'm concerned.

Next to clear weather, the second biggest duck hunting curse is overcrowding. Overcrowding is usually predictable as it tends to occur on corresponding days year after year. The hunt days nearest Christmas and the Saturday after Thanksgiving are always crowded. Sometimes it's almost impossible to kill a duck. On these days the best option is to just stay home.

Pheasant season is great if you're hunting pheasants, but it can be the kiss of death if you want to hunt ducks. There's little else that chases ducks off faster than having people out walking around the refuge. I'd recommend duck hunting on refuges that allow pheasant hunting only after the pheasant season is over. The other alternative is to hunt pheasants. The incompatibility of duck and pheasant hunting is most evident on those refuges that allow pheasant and duck hunting in the same parts of the refuge. There are plenty of refuges that don't allow pheasant hunting. If you want to hunt pheasants, there is good pheasant hunting on several of the refuges, but that's a different subject.

It's the potential for having a very good or very bad day on any particular trip, that makes duck hunting so interesting. If it were a cinch to get a bunch of ducks every time out, duck hunting would loose a great deal of appeal. There's a lot of enjoyment to be had by just being outdoors, getting the exercise, and breathing the fresh air. The duck hunter who measures his pleasure by the number of ducks killed, will always have many unhappy days.

Closing Day At Los Banos

My motivation to hunt ducks was low. I was very tired and feeling the residual effects of being quite cold. It was Saturday, January tenth, 1987 and the evening before the last day of duck season. I had hunted all day with no success. It had been quite cold and my plan for "knocking them dead" on the last weekend at Los Banos Wildlife Area had failed miserably. I had decided that a good hunt was needed to round out my season, and I had been certain that two limits of ducks was what would do the trick. The extra impetus for success had put a little extra pressure on me as the hunter, and along with other uncontrollable factors had contributed to a lack of visible results. Now my thoughts for Sunday were clouded. Should I even bother? Maybe I should drive up to the delta and hunt with my brother and friends on our own property where I suspected that they were having the best shoot of the year.

As I warmed up and relaxed, the thought of returning to the location of the Saturday hunt began to make sense. Actually the pond had been fine. The problem had been with my approach. I'd met a hunter named Tom in the parking lot on Friday night and when we ran into each other again out in the dark along a levee, we decided that it would be advantageous to join forces and hunt over a larger decoy spread. By the time I was ready for bed my resolution was made. It would be interesting to find out how the second day would go, and it had been fun hunting with Tom who was quite avid in his approach.

The decision to go back to the same pond and to hunt with Tom again was fueled by my desire to prove the spot as good as my original impression of it led me to believe it was. In refuge duck hunting it's almost always easier, but not necessarily better hunting, to continue hunting a known spot than to search for a new one. In this particular case there was justification for thinking that the pond could produce ducks, and it would be interesting to see if a few changes in layout and hunting positions would make a significant difference in our success.

I wanted to try hunting a relatively deep and tule surrounded pond a few yards south of the previous day's setup. Tom decided to hunt from the same blind that he had used on Saturday, mainly because he had dogs and needed dry ground for them to lie down on. Standing in waist deep water was okay for a couple of hours, but I reached the point of needing a dry blind by 10 a.m. I had shot at only one duck, a drake sprig that had gone down in the tules and escaped despite the help of Tom and his dogs. That was a second good reason to find a different spot. I had been overly optimistic about my ability to keep ducks from escaping in the tules and didn't want to lose any more birds.

A major problem the day before had been that the ducks had seen me in the tules just as they came into range, and they had continually flared just before the shot. This had led to much frustration and many missed shots. This time I selected a different patch of tules for my blind. They were a better color to blend in with, taller, and thicker. While I was away, Tom had shot at several ducks and had killed a teal and drake sprig. With the decoys placed and new blind established, we settled in and waited to see what the ducks would do.

Ducks were quite active. Many flocks of sprig passed overhead. We imitated teal, widgeon and sprig with whistles. Tom's blind was located approximately 100 yards southwest of mine. Three spoonbill came in over the decoys from the south and turned. They passed directly over Tom. He dropped one on his first shot and missed with his others. A while later, two sprig worked in from the east. When they passed directly over, I was able to drop the hen. It always seems that trends start with the first few shots of the day. I was trying to shoot fewer shots and have a higher percentage of hits. A group of sprig was next. As they came in over Tom's decoys, he opened up but failed to down a bird. As they flared over me, I hit a drake on the first shot, but failed to hit it again and it flew out of sight to the east, limping. I was upset at the inability to kill cleanly and wished that I had resisted the temptation to shoot the long range shot. Two widgeon came in from the west and a drake sprig fell in with them. As the drake approached, Tom unloaded and hit him. I finished him off as he nearly escaped. Frustrated, I pleaded with Tom to let the birds come in closer. He heard my complaint and let a drake sprig pass so that I could take an even better shot at about thirty yards. Now that was more like it!

The high fog threatened to break and the birds continued to work. There were only a few other hunters in the area and they weren't interfering with us at all. It seemed that limits of ducks would be in order as the hunting would only get better as more hunters departed. A large group of teal dropped in over Tom and he fired three shots with no success. I picked off one as he passed over high. A lucky shot, but for some reason I was on target today and so far had hit all six ducks that I'd shot at.

I could tell that Tom was feeling hard pressed. I knew well how it felt to miss ducks. When another group of ducks came in, Tom fired again and was out of shells. I had plenty, so I gave him three of mine. No sooner had I set up again in the blind when two groups of teal came in low. After they circled and passed within ten feet of me I fired; boom...miss, boom...miss. The teal had put me in my place. A short while later, Tom launched his last three shots at a flock of sprig without success. He wouldn't accept any more shells and departed one duck shy of his limit, but he had definitely gotten his money's worth.

Alone now, I had this area of the refuge to myself. It would be a good time to kill two drake mallards to round out my limit. Eight shells were left and an hour of hunting time. I was pretty sure that the ducks would be flying low with the reduced hunter activity. After helping Tom pick up his decoys, I waded back to my tule blind. The marsh was silent now except for the red–winged blackbirds and coots. An occasional shot could be heard in the distance and by listening closely, another hunter could be heard calling frantically off to the west. The last hour of the duck season had arrived. I was satisfied. I had hunted eighteen wildlife refuges on twenty–five hunts. I had killed enough ducks for this year. The rest were safe from me, at least until next season. I decided to leave before the end of shooting time. It had been a fine season, and killing one or two more ducks wouldn't make it any better.

Comments

It turned out that hunting with Tom gave me an extra insight into a common style of duck hunting. Tom had been successful on previous hunts and killed four ducks on this hunt. Tom's main problem was one that plagues many duck hunters. He couldn't pass up a shot. Once the hunter establishes a pattern of missing ducks, it is very difficult to get back on the right track. That's one of the reasons why it pays to be selective. Tom and I hunted out of separate blinds, which had some advantages, but when I hunt with another hunter, I prefer to hunt out of the same blind. This allows both hunters equal shot opportunity. Usually, when I hunt with my brother, we take turns shooting the first shot. That tends to cut down on shooting at the same bird or rushing shots.

What Goes Around Comes Around

In January 1986, my brother Rob, Fred Hilke, and I hunted on our club in the delta. We took turns hunting out of the best blind on the property while the other person hunted the "goose" pond for snow geese and an occasional duck. The property next door to us has no blinds or method of obtaining water, but sometimes the spill-over from our club will flood a portion of that property and occasionally, the owners give somebody permission to hunt there. Such was the case on this day. In general, we get along with the hunters next door, but, on this day things were not so good. One of the hunters in their group had a cannon and was shooting at every goose or duck that came within 100 yards. He was also continually standing up in the open. We knew from experience that our neighbors would have a tough time killing ducks from their spot as there was poor concealment and it's always tough to shoot when you have to lie down to hide. Things weren't made any better when they proceeded to shoot three white front geese which were out of season at that time.

They almost ruined our day. Fortunately, they left about noon, and we did well after they were gone. We hunted until dusk and had near limits when we reached our boat in the dark. A flashlight shone from the bushes and a game warden stepped out and announced his presence. We make every attempt to follow the regs and had no qualms about showing him our ducks. We were surprised when he asked us to empty our packs and bags, but did so to accommodate him. After he pronounced us "clean," we asked him if he had checked the other hunters. He answered that he had, and he had waited for us because they told him that we were shooting white fronts also. I felt like letting out a cheer upon hearing that they had been pinched; needless to say, we don't look forward to seeing them any more.

The purpose of telling this story is twofold. Many people stay away from refuge hunting because they claim that there are too many discourteous hunters or that there is too much sky scraping. These undesirable events can happen anywhere, not just on refuges. To reduce problems, we must start by being courteous and thoughtful ourselves. Some of the rude things that can be done include: sky scraping, setting up in the path to other hunter's decoys, walking around in the area where others are hunting, and moving in too close to other hunters.

On the other side of the coin, it is also unfair to keep other hunters out of an area larger than what is necessary for the hunters using it. Your favorite spot may also be the favorite spot of many others. Often times it will appear that others are sky scraping when perhaps you are taking the same shots. If the other hunter is still putting decoys out when you're ready to shoot, relax; he wants to hunt too. It's easy to be critical when the other hunter is an unknown quantity. Make an effort to get to know the other hunters that you meet. When faces are tied to the guys hunting next door, you'll automatically be less critical. Don't be too competitive. Start by trying to treat the other hunters the way that you want to be treated. Follow the golden rule. What goes around comes around.

Next Season

During the course of this season, I had to hustle to make it to each refuge for a hunt before the season ran out. By the time each refuge had been hunted, there were only ten days left. There had been much of food for thought in talking with other hunters and seeing situations arise in the fields that were new to me. Many of the opportunities that I spotted went unexplored because I didn't have time to test out my theories and still reach my number one goal of hunting each refuge. I plan on trying some, if not all of these theories in the future, but as a duck hunter you may want to test some of them too.

I'm going to put in for opening day at Tule Lake. I've been told that it's an incredible shoot. I'd also like to hunt the marsh there. I plan on taking my own boat with me for a few days of experimentation. I'm also told that hunting Tule Lake on the ice produces great results for honkers. The lake doesn't always freeze over so this opportunity may not present itself.

I'd like to acquire a layout boat. If I do, it will get tested at Meiss Lake on the Butte Valley Wildlife Area. There are numerous ducks and geese on that lake and, as far as I could tell, it's lightly hunted.

An entire season could be devoted to learning just Mendota Wildlife Area. The terrain is very diverse. The number of hunters that can hunt there on any given day is astounding. Mendota has to have some great "pot holes."

I plan on building or buying a decoy carrier so that I can be the one with the most decoys out, at least once next year. This will be a new experience for me.

I'm going to try to get drawn for Los Banos Wildlife Area and hunt out of spaced blind number five to see if it's as good as I've been told. If I had a young son or brother I'd try for area seven at Los Banos which opens only a few days each season for hunters with juniors only.

Parking lot four at San Luis National Wildlife Refuge is another spot that must be hunted. In order to get in there it's necessary to have reservations and get to the refuge early. I'm going to keep trying.

If I get drawn for Kesterson I'll be on the up-wind edge of the sagebrush on big lake at parking lot two, or maybe at the barrels at the south end of area one on the teal pond.

There's lots of exploring left to be done in the free roam area at Sacramento National Wildlife Refuge. I've yet to see the West end of Gray Lodge.

I'm going to hunt the refuges that remain unknown to me and continue to try out new theories about approaching new areas. I'm going to experiment with portable blinds and probably make a few on the refuge as I've done on our private club, with chicken wire and Johnson grass. I'm going to take my boat out on the San Francisco Wildlife Area and learn a little about bay hunting. The Napa Marsh and Petaluma marsh are other areas that I'd like to see. I'm going to get in at least one hunt on the Sherman Island Wildlife Area, once again using my little Boston whaler. I'll continue to go for the five shot limit of sprig and mallards. Next year should be a busy year.

Wetlands Conservation

By all rights, this book could end here. If it did, a great injustice would be done. Wetlands don't just happen as they did at one time. There is little about wetlands that is important to the average American who is more concerned with day-to-day survival. Those of us that know and love the marsh must take an active part in preserving it, or it will be gone forever. As with all things in our society, there is a price to be paid, and we are fortunate that the framework for maintaining and maybe even improving our wetlands has already been created. There are two organizations that California duck hunters should be familiar with.

Ducks Unlimited is currently celebrating 50 years of wetlands conservation. Their membership totals almost 600,000. Since 1937, DU has constructed approximately 2,800 wildlife habitat projects and has raised more than $340 million dollars for this effort. They have done more to protect wetlands in North America than any other single organization and the best is yet to come.

Ducks Unlimited will soon be opening a construction office in the Sacramento area. The target date for opening this office is July 1987. The office will be staffed by a biologist and support staff with the purpose of conducting wetlands construction projects on the West Coast.

The California Waterfowl Association (CWA) was founded in 1946 and has three primary goals: to preserve and enhance wetlands, to improve the production of waterfowl, and to benefit the sport of waterfowling. They currently manage a statewide research program in cooperation with the California Department of Fish & Game at Grizzly Island in the Suisun Marsh, Mendota in the Grasslands, the Sacramento Valley refuge system and Honey Lake and Ash Creek, an area they were responsible for creating and which they manage under contract with CDF&G. CWA sponsored Proposition 19, an $85 million bond issue, to establish the California Duck

Stamp program, that returns more than $750,000 annually for waterfowl research and habitat improvement projects in California. CWA's emphasis on research has been designed to complement the work of other waterfowl groups, such as Ducks Unlimited.

If you are a serious duck hunter, membership in both of these organizations should be a prerequisite to shooting your first duck each season. I've always been suspicious of large fund raising groups, but the people I've met in both of these organizations have impressed me as the type that I'd like to hunt with. They use money wisely.

What Others Have To Say

After the duck season was over and the manuscript for this book was nearly complete, I began to think about ideas for additions to the book which would add value and a little variety. I wanted to obtain information from some other sources, so I contacted John Cowan. I had been introduced to John during the first trip to Gray Lodge. Discussions with John led me to Bill Fischer, and Bill led me to Ray Burmaster. An article in *Western Outdoor News* disclosed Dennis Ludington's phone number. Now they are part of this book, and they have some good advice about hunting and conservation.

(Left to Right) Dan Freeman, Ray Burmaster and Bill Hartman are shown here following a successful hunt that took place during the 1967 season. Photo courtesy of John Cowan.

John A. Cowan

 John Cowan has been at the forefront of refuge management for about forty years. He earned a degree in biology from Chico State College in 1942. During World War II, he became a Navy fighter-dive bomber pilot and flight instructor. Following military service, he did graduate studies in Wildlife Management at UC, Berkeley, leading to a Master's Degree.

The next step in John's career was a game biologist position as Assistant Project Leader on the state's pheasant research project. He was promoted to manager of the 2500 acre Gray Lodge Refuge in November 1947. Over the years, under Cowan's guidance, Gray Lodge Wildlife Area was enlarged to its present size of 8400 acres. He therefore was involved in most of the area's major planning and development.

Cowan also became a prominent member of the Gridley and Butte County community raising a family of two sons and two daughters. He was supported in all his endeavors by his wife, Avis, also a graduate biologist.

Several of John's articles have been published in *Outdoor California*. He is also an award winning photographer. Although he is now retired from the Department of Fish and Game, he is still an active supporter of wetlands and marsh development. John spends a great deal of time in communication with various entities involved in marsh protection, such as the California Wetlands Foundation, Ducks Unlimited and the California Waterfowl Association.

From 1981 to 1983, John was chairman of the Sacramento Valley Waterfowl Habitat Management Committee, a group of conservation minded individuals from diverse backgrounds who produced a plan of action for the U.S. Fish and Wildlife Service and the Department of Fish and Game to promote the protection of wetlands and waterfowl habitat. Since 1900, wetlands have been on the decline in California. At the turn of the century there were approximately four million acres of wetlands in California. As of today the total is less than 300,000 acres. This decline has continued to be evident in more recent times. Even in the premiere duck hunting areas of the Colusa Basin and the Butte Sink, wetlands have declined from a total of about 33,000 acres in 1952, to about 12,000 acres in 1986. Further information on this subject and recommendations for solving problems can be found in *Pacific Flyway Waterfowl in California's Sacramento Valley Wetlands.* This report is the result of the two-year study of the committee which Cowan chaired. I met with John at his home and asked him several questions that I felt would be of interest to the readers of this book. His answers follow:

Q: John, What is it about Gray Lodge Wildlife Area that sets it apart from most other wildlife areas?

A: Each wildlife area has its own special aspects and features. During late November, December and January, Gray Lodge generally has the highest numbers of waterfowl found anywhere on the North American continent. Its location, near the heart of the Pacific Flyway and adjacent to the Butte Sink, accounts for this. Also, hunting activity drives birds into Gray Lodge, where good marshes await.

Gray Lodge is the most intensively developed marshlands wildlife area in the nation. It has good soils. There are 22 major deep well pumps and 20 low lift pump units, with over 100 manageable pond and field units. This is important because water and the ability to move it is the number one requirement of an area such as Gray Lodge. Adequate water has also made possible the development of good riparian and other habitats on the area, in addition to the ponds and marsh areas. This provides a greater variety of

wildlife species than is generally found on most wildlife areas.

Q: Did you undertake special programs to improve the habitat
at Gray Lodge?

A: Habitat improvement and development was a continuing
endeavor. For many years we worked in coordination
with the U.S. Soil Conservation Service and the
Department of Fish and Game's marsh and upland
habitat studies project. We concentrated on develop-
ing diversity of habitat. I believe this was a major
factor in our success. It was also an advantage to
have one person in charge for a long period of time.
There are many subtle changes that occur in the
marsh that can only be identified and understood by
long term observation and management. I think Gray
Lodge benefited from consistent management. I must
also add that I had some outstanding staff people
assist me over the years.

Q: Do you have any tips for hunting Gray Lodge that could
be beneficial to the reader?

A: Good hunting locations on Gray Lodge change constantly.
Knowing what questions to ask at the checking station may help you find a good spot. For example,
where were large numbers of waterfowl feeding the
last few days? These pond areas usually provide good
hunting on the first shoot day following their heavy
bird use. Where are the ponds that are kept flooded
all year? These pond areas generally provide better
shooting than fall-flooded ponds. Apparently, re-
occurring waterfowl food such as duckweed,
pondweed and more numerous invertebrates lure
birds back to the permanent water ponds.

You should also study the area's ponds and their
characteristics as well as the normal flight patterns
around those ponds. This may help increase the
number of birds bagged.

Q: What other types of activities do you suggest that people participate in at wildlife refuges?

A: Nature hikes are my favorite activity. The hiker must keep in mind though that any adverse encroachment on nesting birds or animal dens can have an impact. Restricted areas must be respected; rules must be followed. I'm in favor of firm regimentation in order to minimize the negative impact on wildlife and still maximize visitor enjoyment of the area.

Relatively good fishing is available on most wildlife areas. Birdwatching and general sight-seeing are ever popular activities. Photography and wildlife study are also enjoyable.

Q: While managing the refuge did you take time to hunt?

A: Yes, particularly during my early years at Gray Lodge. I know the excitement that comes to a duck hunter. However, as I became older and lived with the ducks more, I changed from being an avid hunter to being more satisfied with just enjoying the diversity of wildlife found in the marsh. My hunting activity gradually evolved into a major hobby of photography— capturing wildlife, particularly waterfowl, on film.

Q: Were there spots that were consistently good hunting year after year?

A: Yes. Those marsh areas that were maintained as permanent ponds. They provide more continuing diversity of plant and invertebrate waterfowl food which tends to attract ducks. Pass shooting, of course, is consistently better along the closed sanctuary boundary.

Q: Were there any common misconceptions about refuge hunting that you noticed?

A: I think that there is a misconception that hunting on refuges may not be safe. During my time on the refuge, I can say that we had an excellent safety record with no serious accidents. Credit, however, should perhaps go to the state's hunter safety training program.

Q: Do you recall any events that were particularly amusing?

A: Once, when I kicked a hunter out of a no hunting area, he commented that he'd be happy to see me at his place of work. I later found out that he was a guard at Folsom Prison.

Q: Were there common mistakes that hunters made that hindered their success?

A: The biggest problem that I observed was hunters who could not or would not stay put long enough to give the birds a chance to work into the ponds and decoys. Unfortunately, this affected not only their hunting, but also the success of others around them.

Q: Were programs used at Gray Lodge that would be successful on other refuges?

A: There is no minimum requirement for the amount of permanent marsh on each refuge. Some wildlife areas maintain little or none. It is my opinion that the most important function of the wildlife refuges is to provide some permanent stable water ponds in order to sustain the variety of wildlife that is dependent on marsh habitat. Marsh habitat and wildlife are in a drastically declining state. I believe that not less than ten percent of a waterfowl area should be in permanent ponds.

Some areas have agricultural leases that benefit farmers, but not wildlife. The refuges are for wildlife and wildlife should come first. I also feel that, at times, there should be more control over visitors, especially during nesting season. When waterfowl nests or bird rookeries are subject to excessive pressure from intruders, they are often abandoned. If birds abandon a nesting area, they may not find another suitable one and a breeding season may be lost for an entire colony.

In a broader view, I would hope that more wildlife areas would put greater effort into increasing the diversity of their habitat so that it can be beneficial to a broader spectrum of wildlife species. I wish that decisions would be made on the criteria of what is best for waterfowl and other wildlife, rather than what is politically expedient or as a result of public use pressures.

Q: You have witnessed a forty year span of wetlands management and change. Judging from your experience, what do you foresee as the future of our wetlands and waterfowl?

A: I have some good feelings about the future of our waterfowl resource, but also some apprehensions and concerns. We are at a crossroads with the resource. What roads of preservation and resource management we take can tip the scales of the future.

Good hunting in the future will continue to be dependent on the amount and quality of our wintering ground wetlands. Good waterfowl marsh areas have decreased alarmingly in California during the past 40-plus years. Land developments for maximum agricultural use, along with greater call for and cost of water supplies has had major effects on California's waterfowl. Although there has been a significant decrease in waterfowl numbers coming to California during the past 12-15 years (an approximate 30 percent decrease), the major breeding grounds in Alaska and Canada apparently have not been overly affected. Since Pacific Flyway waterfowl have experienced population fluctuations in the past, it may not be overly optimistic to expect a return to higher numbers coming down than at present.

Much has been learned about individual waterfowl species over the years, yet much is not fully understood. Concrete answers to our broad waterfowl population changes are not readily available.

There are many good things starting to occur that can have good positive effects. Waterfowl hunters, managers, administrators, conservationists and the general public are beginning to work together better than ever before in a combined effort to assist wildlife.

Professionals in the field are now focusing more on waterfowl wintering grounds ecology, a subject neglected in the past, primarily due to lack of funding.

Many prominent private duck club owners are doing more to improve the quality of their marshes as well as setting aside or enlarging existing sanctuary areas on the clubs.

The recent strong passage by the general public of a statewide Wetlands Bond issue is another heartening sign to conservationists. It means the majority of Californians want to see our wetland resources preserved. Hopefully, legislators will take heed and become more supportive of wetland conservation measures in the future.

Except during major winter storms and flooding, wintering ground waterfowl are found primarily concentrated on state and federal refuges. There is a need for better dispersement of these birds. Therefore, the major concern is the preservation, acquisition, and recapture of good marshlands habitat. This can be accomplished through easements, subsidies, and acquisition through the public trust and other suitable methods of providing wetlands wildlife with living quarters.

If the above activities and efforts of many continue to grow and if diligent management can prevail, then California's waterfowl resource can be with us for a long time to come.

Ray Burmaster

Ray Burmaster has more information about Region II (refuge) duck hunting at his command than any other independent hunter in Northern California. Over the last two and a half decades he has saved data and plotted the results as only an engineer could. When it comes to performance records, nothing is left to speculation. When I met with Ray at his home, his organization was evident when he led me to his "duck room" where the important items of his hunts were carefully stored, ready for next season. He described his home-made decoy carrier and how he had modified it so that his twelve year old lab could get onto it easier. (He uses the carrier as a platform for the dog while hunting in deep water.) He showed me a couple of pictures of limits of ducks taken during times when he still had hair on his head. I left Ray a list of questions and a draft of this book; he responded with a letter a few days later. (Along with forty-one recommendations for changes in the text. Most of them were used.) His comments are the result of our discussions.

Q: Why do you like to hunt on wildlife refuges when the alternative (hunting on private property where the access is controlled) would appear to be more likely?

A: The main reason is that the birds are migratory. By belonging to a club, you are totally dependent upon the birds being in the area. I generally start the season at the northeastern end of the state and work my way into the Sacramento Valley as the season progresses. The second reason is financial. There are many clubs one can join at a reasonable cost; however, it is very expensive to join a club that will provide shooting as good or better than the public areas. Another reason is that I like to jump shoot and most clubs are too small to allow this.

In addition, I've made a lot of good friends over the years and I enjoy hunting with them.

Q: Do you think that the refuges as a resource are used to their fullest extent?

A: No I don't. There is a significant amount of public area that is underdeveloped. With the shortage of suitable private habitat development, it is essential that the refuges run at maximum efficiency. I do feel that we have a hunting program that is very close to optimum when considering the other constraints.

Q: What is your background and how did you get started as a duck hunter?

A: I have been employed by Aerojet Tactical Systems Company for 29 years, primarily in engineering design and management of small tactical solid rocket motors.

I began hunting at the age of five, using a BB gun. I advanced to small game and then ducks, which I hunted along the San Joaquin Valley drainage ditches.

Later my involvement in refuge hunting problems led me to write to Bill Fischer, then a member of the Sacramento Valley Waterfowl Habitat Management Committee. Because of this involvement, John Cowan asked me to be a committee advisor on refuge hunting and associated problems. While in this advisory position, I met Bill Griffith from the DFG. At the time he was chairman of the Sacramento Valley Waterfowl Advisory Committee. He asked me to serve on his committee. Currently, I am a member of both committees.

Q: Which refuges do you hunt on and which is your favorite, if any? When you decide to hunt a particular refuge, what are generally the reasons behind your selection?

What sources of information do you use to support your decision?

A:I try to get in at least 30 shoot days a season. If drawn, I start the season at Lower Klamath and usually spend the rest of the time in Region II. If I don't get drawn for the season opener in Region II, I will usually go to the grassland refuges,if drawn. If not drawn for either, I'll get in the first–come–first–served line at one of the Region II wildlife areas. If the season is delayed in Region II due to a late rice harvest, I will hunt the grassland refuges, usually Volta. My favorite Region II wildlife areas are Colusa and Sutter. I usually start hunting one of them in mid–season. Sutter has the best mallard hunting when compared to the other areas. There are several factors that I consider in refuge selection for a specific day hunt. They include; the time of year, the hunter bag average, the predicted weather, the major duck species being taken, and the likelihood of being admitted prior to shooting time. Making this decision requires constant surveillance of data released by DFG and continuous conversations with other public area hunters.

Q: Do you have some specific tips to offer in the use of decoys, setting up, calling, shooting or retrieving?

A: There are many articles published about the use of decoys so I'll not spend too much time on it. The most common placement that I use on big spreads, is similar to an "O" with the center open, the sides filled and a single row on the top and bottom. In public area hunting it is very important where your decoys are placed in relation to the other hunter around you. You should try and make the other hunter's decoys work to your advantage without infringing upon his hunt. The major thing to avoid is to have another hunter set up directly down wind of you. I have found that a pleasant conversation with my neighbors prior to shooting time is well worth the effort in that it creates a work together atmosphere rather than a competitive event that can end in a shouting match. If your neighbor doesn't have a dog, volunteer to bring yours over to help him find his lost birds. A lot of people that I hunt with today are people that I met in friendly conversations prior to shooting time. The number of decoys that I use varies considerably. In hunting over decoys last year the smallest number that I used was eight mallards and the largest number was fourteen dozen mallards and pintail. It all depends on where I'll be shooting, the weather, the type bird I would like to bag and the number of hunters in the group. I prefer to hunt with one other person, but sometimes hunt with three if I'm with a group of friends.

Q: Having reviewed my book draft, what important details would you like to add or emphasize?

A: After setting up, move around until you are standing under the place where the birds are flying the lowest. This may or may not be at the upper end of the decoys. Lots of times I leave the decoys entirely and move upwind of them. This works best on high-wind days late in the season when the birds are wary.

I think the book should place a more positive emphasis on the use of dogs. Too many birds are not recovered by hunters after being downed in thick cover. I will hardly go hunting without my dog because she is that much help. She spots the birds behind me that I can't see and finds birds that I could never hope to find. I never let her stay in cold water that touches her chest. To keep her out of the water I assemble four short pieces of PVC pipe into a square. This fits nicely inside a decoy bag that is cinched up and placed on some folded over tules. It works just like a trampoline. She is getting old, so I started training a new pup last season.

I'd like to see more in the book about jump shooting, pass shooting (particularly about shooting the firing line at Delevan) and alternative hunting opportunities for species such as pheasant and snipe. On a slow day I like to swap my twelve gauge with duck loads, for my twenty gauge with #9 shot. This can turn a disastrous duck hunt into a fine snipe shoot. They are fast, hard to hit, and create a pleasant challenge.

Q: As a representative for hunters on the committee which makes recommendations for changes in refuge management, how do you determine what is in the best interest of the refuges and the hunter?

A: This is a tight rope. My annual report is based upon my observations and discussions with other hunters. For instance the use of bicycles in the hunting area became an item of concern to some of the hunters. To find out how hunters felt about this, I interviewed approximately 100 hunters in four different areas. In addition, a report draft is circulated through approximately twenty dedicated refuge hunters prior to submittal. Since the hunters that I am able to interview are usually in the first half of the first-come-first-served line and may not represent the majority opinion on close issues, I will not recommend a change unless there is a large margin in its favor. A recommendation may be further tempered by talking to DFG personnel, an assessment of the effect on habitat, and other knowledge which I have gained while working on the two committees.

Q: What types of habitat do you prefer to find on a refuge? Why?

A: I normally hunt the natural marsh areas. For mallards I use a small number of decoys in a small opening on a large tule covered pond. For sprig I hunt more open water and put out all the decoys I can carry. There is a necessity to have other kinds of cereal types of crops for duck food. I usually by-pass these because they do not provide adequate hunter concealment. If there is high use by the ducks, they may be successfully hunted in these areas despite poor concealment.

Q: Have you noticed trends in refuge duck hunting that are an indication of what's in store for the future?

A: With the very limited private marshlands today, the duck picture is not very bright. I think that the California Waterfowl Association is doing an excellent job trying to turn things around; however, they are a relatively small organization and could use more Ducks Unlimited and government help. I also get the feeling that Ducks Unlimited is more interested in the eastern half of the country even though we are a major contributor to their funding. They need to do a lot of fence mending on the west coast. They have started on this task.

I started refuge hunting in the early 1950's; however, my refuge hunting data base only goes back to 1960, so the following comments are based from 1960 until now. There has been a general decline in the hunter's bag on the Sacramento, Gray Lodge, and Sutter areas. Colusa and Delevan have actually improved during this time frame. The more recent data indicated that all are tending to level out with a somewhat reduced bag at Sacramento, Gray Lodge, and Sutter. In general, our duck hunting has held up quite well when you consider the decline in the duck population. This is probably because, with the disappearance of private wetlands, the remaining ducks don't have many options on where to stay.

Dennis Ludington

I found out about Dennis by reading *Western Outdoor News*.

The author of the article had hunted with Dennis at San Luis Wildlife Refuge and was impressed by the action. He quoted Dennis as saying that it was amazing to him that more people didn't take advantage of refuge hunting. At that point, I had the urge to question Dennis about his methods, but it wasn't until later on (after I decided to do these interviews) that I actually called him and pursued the opportunity. Dennis makes a living as the owner of and trainer at PACIFIC FLYWAY KENNELS near Los Banos. From Dennis's home you can almost see the ducks working at Volta Wildlife Refuge.

Q: Why do you like to guide hunts on wildlife refuges when the alternative (hunting on private property where the access is controlled) would appear to be more likely?

A: I think that the refuges attract ducks much as other large bodies of water do, and act like a holding area. For this reason there are almost always plenty of ducks there.

Q: Do you think that the refuges as a resource, are used to their fullest extent?

A: I think that the refuges could be better utilized in the off season. Several times I've had refuge managers say to me that they can't afford to have too many people utilizing the refuge for fishing or dog training because there's no funds for road repair. A reasonable fee should be charged for access to the areas and in this manner revenue will be generated to cover the operational cost. Currently, there's no fee that I know of for fishing, birding or dog training. I don't think that it's reasonable to expect to do these things for free.

I also think that, as a general comment, more should be done by management to keep the refuge in the type of habitat that is best for the biggest variety of birds. Each refuge manager seems to have types of habitat that they personally prefer. When they arrive they tend to try to replace existing habitat with their personal favorite. I think that the habitat should be tailored to the refuge and its "personality." Each refuge is different and should have its own special type of habitat, not something brought in from elsewhere.

For example, there's great watergrass habitat at Mendota. In cold weather the ducks love it. It provides feed and also cover from the wind. I like hunting watergrass at Mendota, but I don't want to see the tules ripped out at Los Banos and replaced with watergrass!

Q: What is your background and how did you get started as a guide?

A: My background is as a professional dog trainer and I guide because I enjoy it and it's part of dog training. I train retrievers for field trials and as gun dogs. Duck hunting is very closely associated to the training.

Q: Which refuges do you guide on and which is your favorite, if any?

A: I guide mainly on San Luis and Mendota, and Mendota is my favorite. Mendota is a tremendous refuge and well managed. There is a tremendous variety of habitat. Some areas of the refuge are great for sprig while others are better for a variety of birds.

Q: Do you have some specific tips to offer in the use of decoys, setting up, calling, shooting or retrieving?

A: On decoys I'd say that most hunters "overdecoy." I've probably shot more birds over a half–dozen to a dozen decoys than over large spreads. It doesn't normally pay to use a large number of decoys. If it's a slow day with no wind, then a bunch of lifeless decoys sitting motionless on a pond may be less natural looking than just a few decoys. If you've got a good stormy day with lots of wind (where the decoys look the best), it's usually good enough hunting that you don't need a whole bunch of decoys anyway. Occasionally, we'll put out a lot of decoys, especially if hunting for sprig on a large pond. If you hunt big water for sprig, then you have to have more decoys.

I use face camo so that I can watch the birds when they're working. I never take my eyes off a bird once it starts working and I never pass up singles in hopes of getting a shot at more than one bird.

On shooting, I'd say that for years I tended to shoot in front of birds. Now I try to load fast shells and vary the load so that the speed of my shot will be the same no matter whether I'm shooting my twenty gauge with standard loads or magnum loads. I shoot at a birds nose or just a few inches in front of the bird and seem to do okay. I use a gun with a 26 inch barrel. The short barrel is a lot easier to use.

I usually hunt from further down wind that most hunters. I try to shoot at birds from a position where there's lots of room between me and the decoys for the birds to work. Often times I'll be hunting from dry ground. There are places I hunt where the birds work better over the dry ground than over the water.

On calling, I'd say that its very important to call well. It takes practice, but there's few reasons why everybody can't learn to be a good caller. I recommend two calls, the Yensen double reed call (which is only about $12) and the Paul Kinsyon call (which is about a $70 call). I think the Kinsyon call is the best on the market. It's easy to blow and comes properly tuned.

Q: Having reviewed my book draft, what important aspects of the hunt did I overlook or underestimate?

A: Some of the items on your equipment list are worth mentioning. Wool is very important for shirts, trousers, socks and gloves. A compass is an item that can be quite valuable.

I place a great deal of importance on having a good retriever. With a good dog one should almost never lose birds that go down in sight.

Q: How do you feel about the problems created by dog use that I mention in the book, such as dog fights?

A: You can learn to spot potential dog fights. They usually occur when one dog owner doesn't have control of his dog. Watch for that situation and avoid that individual.

Q: Should a dog be allowed to stand in the water while you're hunting.

A: There are some times of the early season when it's warm out and it may be okay to have your dog stand in the water, but late in the season when it gets cold, you should never allow your dog to be exposed to this type of cold. Find dry ground or make a platform for the dog to stand on. Hypothermia can effect dogs just like people.

Q: What other advice do you have for dog owners?

A: Make sure your dog is prepared for the hunt. Train properly, especially obedience training. Feed the dog proper high protein food during the hunting season and bring along a high energy snack for the dog. If you have a young dog in his first year of hunting, it will probably be best to keep him on a leash when travelling to and from the hunt.

Q: What types of habitat do you prefer to find on a refuge? Why?

A: I prefer tules because almost all varieties of ducks can be found there. You'll seldom get skunked if you hunt in tule areas. You'll get mallards, gadwall, teal, shovelers, widgeon and often sprig too. If you hunt big open water ponds, then you'll be limited to sprig, widgeon, or shovelers and have a greater chance of not getting your ducks.

Q: Have you noticed trends in refuge duck hunting that are an indication of what's in store for the future?

A: There's a definite trend towards improved equipment and technology. As hunters seek out better technology, it will become more difficult to be successful unless you also improve. The guy who rides a bicycle in the dark to his hunt location will almost always beat the guy on foot. In order to remain competitive each hunter will have to be better at what he does.

Dennis Ludington trains retrievers and also guides at San Luis N.W.R. and Mendota W.A. This photo was taken after a 1986 hunt. Photo courtesy of Dennis Ludington.

Bill Fischer

 Bill Fischer is an avid duck hunter. He began hunting refuges in 1955 at Grizzly Island. These were the days when you had to take the ferry across Montezuma Slough, six cars at a time. During the 1956 season he hunted at Gray Lodge for the first time. He still hunts Grizzly Island in the early season, but switches to Gray Lodge after the first few weeks. To Bill, it's the setting of Gray Lodge with the Sutter Buttes as a backdrop, that sets it apart from other refuges. With the decline of the sprig population over recent years, Bill says that the early season limits of "fat Grizzly Island sprig" are a thing of the past, but with the upswing of the mallard population, he still manages to get some nice bunches of big birds.

It was at Gray Lodge that Bill became friends with John Cowan, as well as many other regulars at the refuge. In fact, when reviewing the story about opening day at Gray Lodge, he knew from my descriptions many of the people I had met.

Q: Bill, why do you like to hunt on wildlife refuges?

A: The main reason that I've stayed with refuge hunting is that I've met and continue to meet such a diversity of people on the refuges. "Each year I look forward to seeing friends again–"; Bob and Edie (whose two Griffins are gone; Edie now has a beautiful Chesapeake)..., big Paul the "Sea Captain"..., the "Russians"..., San Francisco Mike..., Monterey Mike..., Gene, Borris and the others; Ron "The Mallard Man" (with his black Lab)..., Tom Crawford and his "cooking camp" under the blue tarp where his hospitality is open to all during the week before duck and later pheasant season,...he has put on some great feeds.

A second reason that I enjoy the wildlife refuges is that I can hunt a variety of habitat and different areas at a reasonable expense. Duck hunting isn't an inexpensive sport, but at the refuges the cost is certainly much less than at private clubs.

Although I don't do it as much as I used to, the ability to go from refuge to refuge in order to be where the hunting is "hot," is a big advantage. On a private club you're restricted to one spot and if the birds aren't there for a few weeks, your only option is to sit and enjoy the solitude until the birds return.

Q: What is your background and how did you get started as a duck hunter?

A. My start in duck hunting is unusual in that I don't come from a family with a hunting background. I started duck hunting with my father–in–law and some of my friends from work. I didn't actually duck hunt until one day I saw a picture of a Browning automatic shotgun in *Field and Stream* and decided that I was going to have to try that. My first gun turned out not to be that browning, but a Winchester model twelve; sixteen gauge, that's still my favorite gun. That first year I hunted exclusively at Grizzly Island. The limit was ten birds and even though I wasn't the best shot, I got a few of those Grizzly Island sprig and that got me hooked.

Q: Which refuges do you hunt and which is your favorite, if any?

A: I've hunted on Grizzly Island, the Sacramento Valley complex, Gray Lodge, and a few times at the San Joaquin Valley refuges. The vast majority of my hunting has been at Grizzly Island and Gray Lodge. Over the years, I've enjoyed hunting all the refuges, however, Gray Lodge has been my favorite. It has always been so well managed. The quality of the hunting, and I guess the beautiful setting, keep calling me back.

Bill Fischer (left) and Arch Patterson prepare to head home after a hunt that took place in 1971.

Q: Do you have some specific tips to offer in the use of decoys, setting up, calling, shooting or retrieving?

A. Most of the time I don't use a large number of decoys and I don't think that a large number of decoys is important. I once observed a hunter at Grizzly Island hunting with one large sprig decoy and he was having one of the best shoots I've ever seen. I believe in the mallard call and when used correctly, it is a tremendous asset. If used incorrectly, you can run every duck out of the area. I use a sprig call, but I don't think it is as effective; however, it doesn't run the birds off either. It's pretty hard to blow a sour note or "over call" as is so often done with the mallard call.

When it comes to retrieving, I think that a dog is very important. I used to have an Irish Setter and now I have two Springer Spaniels. Molly, my Irish Setter, could smell a duck a block away, but one problem, she couldn't take the cold water. Twice I literally had to carry her off Gray Lodge with hypothermia. After the second time, I quit taking her in the late season.

Q: Having reviewed my book draft, what important aspects of the refuge hunt did I overlook or underestimate?

A: I think that hunters overlook the value of the afternoon hunt. It's during the afternoon that a hunter can have a lot of room to himself. During these times one can practice calling without interfering with others. Many times the ducks work better in the afternoon when most of the hunters have gone home.

I think that simplifying and standardizing regulations on the various refuges, to the extent that it's possible, would be a good idea. I like the option of using a travel-trailer at Gray Lodge and would like to see that opportunity offered at other refuges. I think that it's very important to ask as many questions as possible of the Department of Fish and Game officials to learn about changes in refuge habitat, bird concentrations and anything else that comes to mind. They have always been very co-operative and helpful to me.

I'd like to elaborate on a couple of aspects of retrieving. It has been my experience that if a duck dives, it's important to stay still and watch for bubbles in the water. Often this will give them away in their attempt to escape by swimming under water. I've made it my golden rule to go after every duck hit and make every effort to get him. I just hate to loose a cripple.

When two people hunt together its important that both go after downed ducks. With both hunters converging on the bird from different directions, the chances of locating the bird are greatly increased, especially when hunting in heavy cover such as tules or the marsh grass at Grizzly Island.

In order to mark the maximum range that I'm going to shoot I'll put a decoy or other marker at about forty yards to make recognizing the range easier. When standing up to shoot, it helps to raise up slowly so that the birds won't flair.

Generally, I think it makes a lot of sense to use more drake decoys than hens; first, because they show up better and secondly, drakes far outnumber hens in the early season, particularly with the pintail species.

As far as waders, I prefer the Super Seal Dry 100's with tennis shoes, mainly because they are easy to walk in. I know there are many other good brands, but I have worn these for years with good success.

For years when hunting Gray Lodge, I felt that if I couldn't get on the "West Side" it wasn't worth going. Then one afternoon in 1965 or 1966, Ed Ratterman and I didn't get on until after 3 p.m. on Saturday and had to go "East." We checked off at the end of shooting time with two very respectable limits of ducks and a goose. Since then we've been going "East." I'm not going to give away my secrets as to just where.........but the "East Side." There are lots of quality spots on the east side just as there are on the west side, but not as much hunting pressure.

Q: You participated in the study called; *PACIFIC FLYWAY WATERFOWL IN CALIFORNIA'S SACRAMENTO VALLEY WETLANDS: AN ANALYSIS OF HABITAT....A PLAN FOR PROTECTION.* What motivated you to spend your time on such a project? Will some of the recommendations of the program be successfully carried out? Do you have some specific ideas for ways that the average waterfowler can contribute to the solution of wetlands problems and waterfowl management?

A: John Cowan had suggested my name to the selection committee, comprised of the members of the U.S Fish and Wildlife Service, the California Department of Fish and Game and a representative of the California Waterfowl Association. Over the years, I had shown a great deal of interest in the operation of Gray Lodge as well as all the refuges I hunted. On occasion I had written letters to the Department suggesting changes in the operation and regulations. Due to the interest I had shown over the years, I was selected to represent the "unaffiliated hunters" as a member of the committee. I welcomed this opportunity as I had a great deal of respect for John and felt that this study would be a real challenge, as it turned out to be. Many of the recommendations that we made have been implemented. Among them was the phasing out of co-operative rice farming and diversifying the refuge habitat more than had been done in the past. In the course of the study, it was brought to our attention that herbicidal spraying for unwanted aquatic growth in rice fields was on occasion being applied carelessly by crop–dusters causing damage to nearby trees and other desirable habitat. We brought this to the attention of the various County Boards of Supervisors where remedial action was immediately taken.

Another of our recommendations, further development of the Oroville Wildlife Areas, is presently becoming a reality with funds and effort being directed toward improving wildlife habitat. This area does have quite a bit of potential with the proper management and development.

Of the sixty–five recommendations made by the committee, certainly a great number of them have already been implemented, but a good majority of them are on–going. Continuous effort must be made over the years to make these recommendations a reality.

Q: What is your wish for the future of California's wetlands and waterfowl?

A: I think we need to encourage the hunter as well as educate him in conservation. Groups such as Ducks Unlimited and the California Waterfowl Association need hunter support.

The Department of Fish and Game and U.S. Fish and Wildlife Service should solicit suggestions from hunters and encourage them to write to their representative in the legislature and Congress on items of mutual importance.

Unfortunately, much anti-hunting sentiment exists on the issue of gun control and also within environmental groups. The refuge user, other than the duck hunter, doesn't pay a fee. The duck hunters financial support is critical to the future development of wildlife habitat and preservation of the habitat we presently have.

For the future I'd like to see more wetlands. I'd like to see a property tax exemption for wetlands which would encourage development of more wetlands by the private sector. Today's agricultural practices have become extremely efficient and often to the detriment of wildlife. Public interest must be stimulated to encourage agricultural business interests to recognize the need to preserve wildlife habitat and incorporate these objectives into their long-term farming plans as well as day-to-day operations.

State and Federal Waterfowl Hunting Areas Covered in this Book

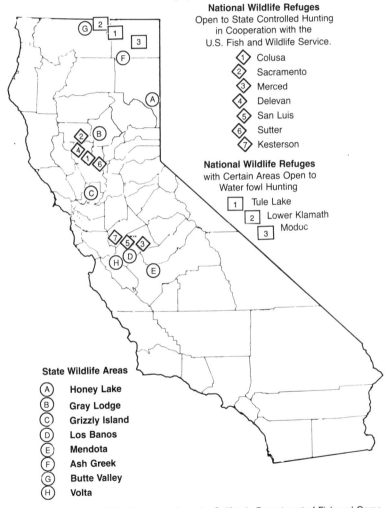

National Wildlife Refuges
Open to State Controlled Hunting
in Cooperation with the
U.S. Fish and Wildlife Service.

1. Colusa
2. Sacramento
3. Merced
4. Delevan
5. San Luis
6. Sutter
7. Kesterson

National Wildlife Refuges
with Certain Areas Open to
Water fowl Hunting

1. Tule Lake
2. Lower Klamath
3. Modoc

State Wildlife Areas

A. Honey Lake
B. Gray Lodge
C. Grizzly Island
D. Los Banos
E. Mendota
F. Ash Greek
G. Butte Valley
H. Volta

Reprinted With Permission from the California Department of Fish and Game
Note: These maps are subject to annual revisions. It is important to obtain an up-to-date map
at the refuge, prior to hunting.

105

Colusa National Wildlife Refuge

Size: 4040 total acres, 1230 huntable acres. Eleven ponds with 970 flooded acres.
Hunter Quota:80
Check In Time: Two hours before shoot time.
Trailers: Not allowed.
Boats: Not allowed.
Hunt Days: Saturday, Sunday and Wednesday.

Recommendations: I hunted here in late November while the hunting was generally slow and was able to get onto the refuge when I arrived at shooting time. During late December and January, non–reservation hunters may need to arrive before noon on Friday to get onto the refuge for the Saturday morning shoot. I had success in the tule marsh to the west of Ohm road. The popular spot was pond six on the east side of the refuge. Top five species harvested as percentage of total 1986/87 duck harvest: 1. Mallard-26%. 2. Widgeon-23%. 3. Greenwing Teal-16%. 4. Gadwall -11%. 5. Pintail-9%. Geese made up approximately 2% of the total of ducks and geese harvested in 1986/87.

Colusa National Wildlife Refuge

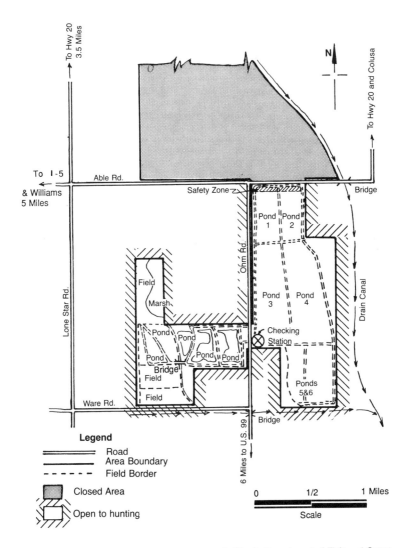

Reprinted With Permission from the California Department of Fish and Game
Note: These maps are subject to annual revisions. It is important to obtain an up-to-date map at the refuge, prior to hunting.

Delevan National Wildlife Refuge

Size: 5634 total acres, 2,250 huntable acres. Fifteen ponds with 1503 flooded acres.
Hunter Quota: 120
Check In Time: Two hours before shoot time.
Trailers: Not allowed.
Boats: Not allowed.
Hunt Days: Saturday, Sunday and Wednesday.

Recommendations: During high use periods non-reservation holders will need to arrive by late afternoon on Friday to hunt Saturday morning. On the day that I hunted Delevan, there were several hunters doing well by hiding in clumps of tules about one half mile northwest of parking lot 3. The wind was out of the northwest that day and the birds were working in over the open water and coming down on the up wind side of the large pond. The prevailing winds here are from that direction so that spot will frequently be good. Delevan is noted for its pass shooting for snow geese. Watching with field glasses is a good way to spot flyways. The geese tend to concentrate in one area of the closed zone and then fly up wind from that spot. Top five species of ducks harvested as a percentage of total 1986/87 duck harvest: 1. Mallard-19%. 2. Greenwing teal-19%. 3. Pintail 17%. 4. Shoveler-16%. 5. Widgeon-16%. Geese made up approximately 7% of the total ducks and geese harvested in 1986/87.

Delevan National Wildlife Refuge

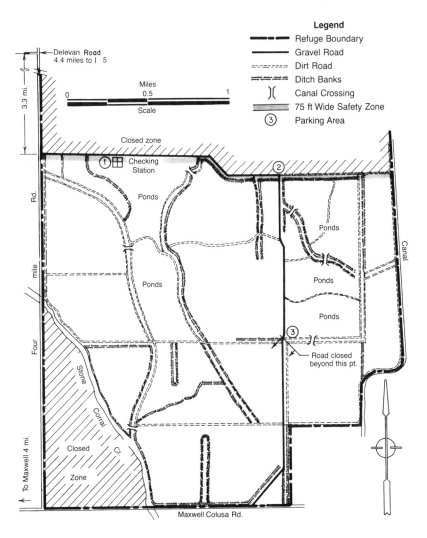

Reprinted With Permission from the California Department of Fish and Game
Note: These maps are subject to annual revisions. It is important to obtain an up-to-date map
at the refuge, prior to hunting.

Gray Lodge Wildlife Area

Size: 8400 acres total, 6,000 acres huntable. Approximately 80 ponds.

Hunter Quota: 400

Check In Time: Two hours before shoot time.

Trailers: Allowed.

Boats: Not allowed.

Hunt Days: Saturday, Sunday and Wednesday.

Recommendations: Gray Lodge is quite large and has beautiful ponds. The West end is most popular because of the closed area and the permanent marsh, but there are regulars that prefer the less crowded east end.

This is a great spot to bring a trailer to and stay for a while. There is plenty of parking space and running water at the refuge. Top five species of duck harvested as a percentage of total 1986/87 duck harvest: 1. Mallard-19%. 2. Greenwing teal-18%. 3. Gadwall-17%. 4. Pintail-17%. 5. Shoveler-12%. Goose harvest approximately 1% of total duck and goose harvest.

Gray Lodge State Wildlife Area

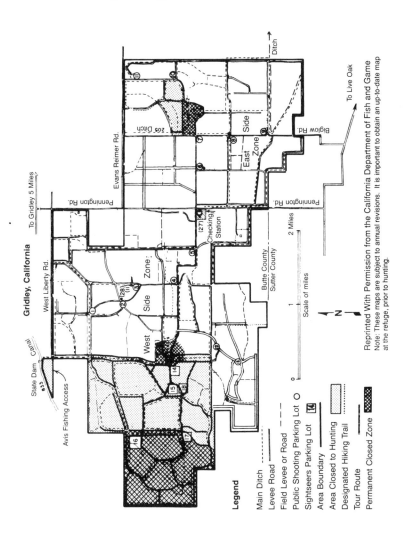

Gridley, California

Reprinted With Permission from the California Department of Fish and Game

Note: These maps are subject to annual revisions. It is important to obtain an up-to-date map at the refuge, prior to hunting.

Legend

Main Ditch

Levee Road

Field Levee or Road

Public Shooting Parking Lot O

Sightseers Parking Lot

Area Boundary

Area Closed to Hunting

Designated Hiking Trail

Tour Route

Permanent Closed Zone

Sutter National Wildlife Refuge

Size: 2591 Total acres, 1295 huntable. Hunter Quota: 80
Check In Time: Two hours before shoot time.
Trailers: Not allowed.
Boats: Not allowed.
Hunt Days: Saturday, Sunday and Wednesday.

Recommendations: I didn't fare well at Sutter, but other hunters that I talked with had done well on Sundays when the number of hunters was down. Hunting inside the by-pass can be tough if there are a large number of hunters there.

The part of the refuge that is outside the by-pass is open fields. Inside the by-pass there is mullet, tule marsh and tree lined canals. This area is one of the best for mallards. Top five species of ducks harvested as percentage of total 1986/87 duck harvest: 1. Mallard-45%. 2. Shoveler-13%. 3. Pintail-12%. 4. Widgeon-11%. 5. Greenwing teal-8%. Goose harvest less than 1% of total duck and goose harvest in 1986/87.

Sutter National Wildlife Refuge

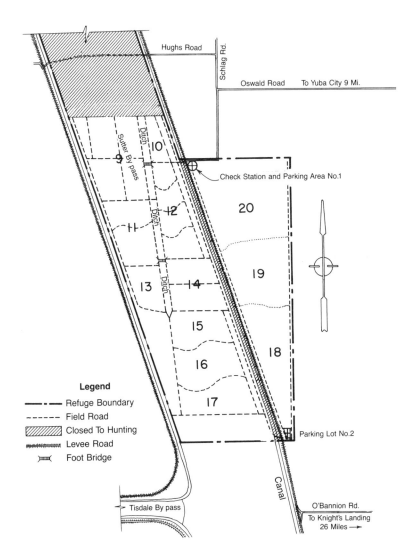

Hughs Road

Schlag Rd.

Oswald Road   To Yuba City 9 Mi.

Sutter By pass

Ditch

9

10

Check Station and Parking Area No.1

12

11

Ditch

20

13   14   Ditch

19

15

16

18

17

Legend

—·—·— Refuge Boundary

– – – – Field Road

▨▨▨ Closed To Hunting

Levee Road

⟩▥⟨ Foot Bridge

Parking Lot No.2

Canal

Tisdale By pass

O'Bannion Rd.

To Knight's Landing
26 Miles →

Reprinted With Permission from the California Department of Fish and Game

Note: These maps are subject to annual revisions. It is important to obtain an up-to-date map at the refuge, prior to hunting.

113

Sacramento N. W. R.

Size: 10,783 acres total with 3969 acres open to hunting.
Hunter Quota: 56 blinds. Also large free roam area.
Maximum possible capacity 264.
Check Out Time: Two hours before shoot time.
Trailers: Not allowed.
BOATS: Not allowed.
Hunt Days: Saturday, Sunday and Wednesday.

Recommendations: There is a large body of water located south of blind 12 which held a large concentration of ducks and geese on the day I hunted at Sacramento refuge. The prevailing winds are out of the north so as the birds lifted off they frequently passed over the area of blind 12. This blind had quite a bit of activity on ducks and geese while others had very little success. The blind that I used here was built inside a tule patch. It was poorly concealed, and there wasn't much that I could do about it. Trial and error is the only way to learn which blinds work. Some of the blinds are barrel blinds.

The blind area has good roads that are easy walking. This provides an opportunity for hunters who cannot traverse rough terrain. This area provides a service to senior citizen duck hunters who aren't ready to give up the hunt. By contacting the refuge in advance, special arrangements can be made to make access available for handicapped individuals. Top blinds in 1986/87 were: 1.#12-97hunters/304ducks 2.#56-104/319 3.#49-102/307 4.#16-118/355 5.#54-92/ 276 6.#41-80/236 7.#50-113/321 8.#19 -50/127 9.#55-86/ 217 10.#45-110/277 11.#4-93/234 12.#7-74/185 13.#36-103/252 14.#32-91/211 15.#43-90/206 16.#1-78/174 17.#48-81/179 18.#31-74/161 19.#11-109/234 20.#29-60/ 127. Top five species of ducks harvested as percentage of total 1986/87 harvest: 1. Mallard-19%. 2. Pintail -19%. 3. Shoveler-16%. 4. Widgeon-15%. 5. Gadwall -15%. Geese made up 8% of the total ducks and geese harvested in 1986/87.

Sacramento National Wildlife Refuge
Hunting From Blind Sites Only

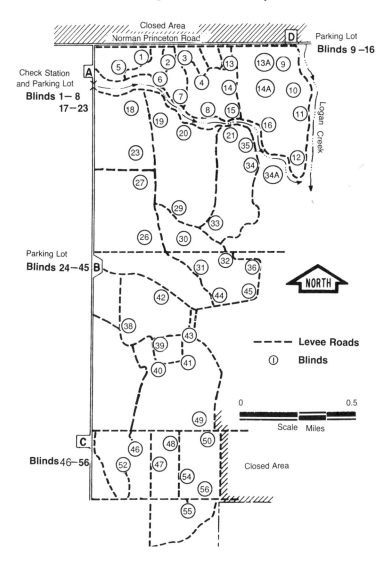

Closed Area
Norman Princeton Road

D Parking Lot
Blinds 9 –16

Check Station
and Parking Lot
**Blinds 1— 8
17—23**

Logan Creek

NORTH

Parking Lot
Blinds 24—45

- - - - **Levee Roads**

① **Blinds**

0   0.5

Scale Miles

Blinds 46—56

Closed Area

Reprinted With Permission from the California Department of Fish and Game
Note: These maps are subject to annual revisions. It is important to obtain an up-to-date map
at the refuge, prior to hunting.

Sacramento National Wildlife Refuge

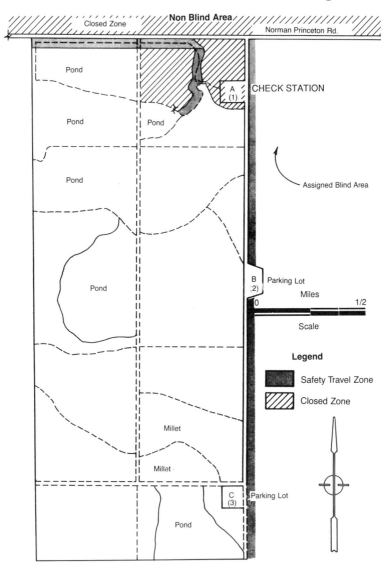

Reprinted With Permission from the California Department of Fish and Game
Note: These maps are subject to annual revisions. It is important to obtain an up-to-date map at the refuge, prior to hunting.

Sacramento Valley Area

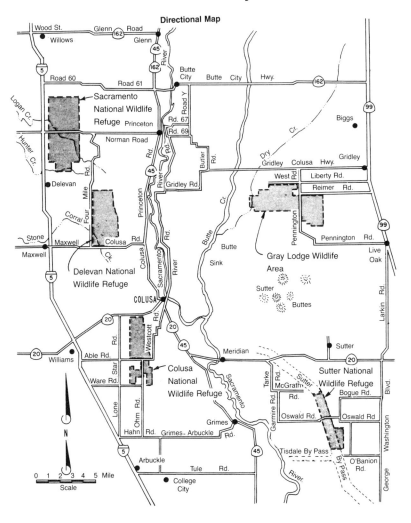

Directional Map

Reprinted With Permission from the California Department of Fish and Game
Note: These maps are subject to annual revisions. It is important to obtain an up-to-date map at the refuge, prior to hunting.

Grizzly Island Wildlife Area

Size: 5700 acres of ponds and 1000 acres of fields open to shooting. Additional 1500 acres of uplands open for the first nine days of pheasant season. Hunter Quota: 350

Check In Time: At least two hours before shooting time.

Trailers: No.

Boats: No.

Recommendations: This is a fair weather refuge. Hunting usually declines in fowl weather or fog. Being a delta/bay refuge, Grizzly Islands best days probably won't coincide with the best opportunities on other refuges. Keep this in mind and you may be able to have a greater number of successful hunts. This is one refuge that I'd avoid during the early part of pheasant season as the ducks get run right out of the area. Hunters are on the refuge every day during the first nine days of pheasant season, and the ducks don't like it.

There are about 17 double barrel blinds in the crescent unit that are quite popular in the later half of the season. You must have at least one dozen decoys to hunt the crescent unit. Best four blinds in the Crescent Unit in 1986/87 were: 1. #5-25hunters/47ducks 2. #15-26/34 3. #13-18/27 4. #12-35/38. Top five species of duck harvested as a percentage of total 1986/87 duck harvest: 1. Mallard-24%. 2. Pintail-22%. 3. Greenwing teal-19%. 4. Shoveler-15%. 5. Widgeon-13%. Goose harvest quite small.

Grizzly Island Wildlife Area

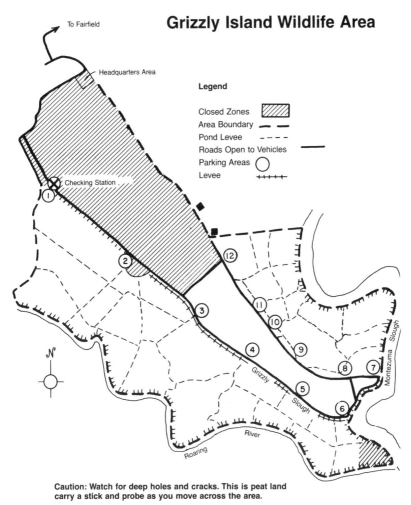

To Fairfield

Headquarters Area

Legend

Closed Zones	
Area Boundary	
Pond Levee	
Roads Open to Vehicles	
Parking Areas	
Levee	

Checking Station

Montezuma Slough

Grizzly Slough

Roaring River

N

Caution: Watch for deep holes and cracks. This is peat land carry a stick and probe as you move across the area.

Reprinted With Permission from the California Department of Fish and Game
Note: These maps are subject to annual revisions. It is important to obtain an up-to-date map at the refuge, prior to hunting.

Crescent Unit

Of the Grizzly Island Wildlife Area

Tree e Slough

Legend

— ·· —	Area Boundary
	Levee
	Ditches
	Access Road
•—	Pole Line
	Ditch Crossing
	Closed Zones
○	Parking Areas
△	Double Duck Blinds
△s	Single Duck Blinds

To Fairfield 9 miles

Grizzly Island Rd

Headquarters

To checking station 2.6 miles

0   1/2

Scale

Reprinted With Permission from the California Department of Fish and Game
Note: These maps are subject to annual revisions. It is important to obtain an up-to-date map
at the refuge, prior to hunting.

San Joaquin Valley

Directional Map

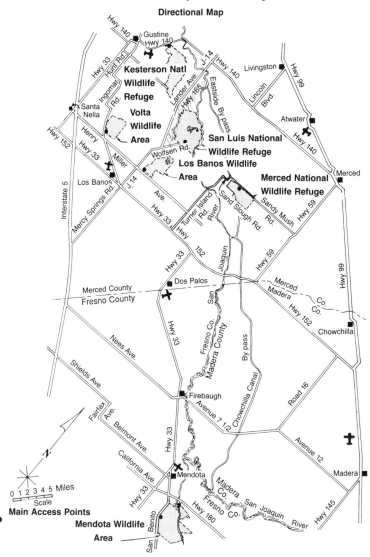

Mendota Wildlife Area

Size: 10,480 acres total, 7900 huntable acres. 45 total ponds.

Hunter Quota: 600. Other than opening weekend of duck and pheasant seasons, Mendota is seldom if ever filled to capacity.

Check In Time: Two hours before shoot time. According to Marci who has worked at the check station for several seasons, it has consistently opened at 3:30 a.m.

Trailers: Not allowed.

Boats: Allowed.

Hunt Days: Saturday, Sunday and Wednesday.

Recommendations: One big advantage of hunting Mendota is that the hunting is good during the entire season. The large amount of water there and the fact that there are not other areas in the same vicinity to compete for birds, tends to keep the hunting consistent. I hunted out of parking lot 18. There were quite a few birds in the area, but also many hunters. As is the norm, only a few locations were getting consistent action. This would be a tough area to break into as the regulars are going to get to the good spots pretty fast. Field 20 was mostly tules in small ponds. Field 17 was large open water ponds with little cover.

Mendota has a wide variety of hunting habitat. It is interesting that boats are allowed for hunting on Fresno Slough. The Tule Island area is also interesting, but I've been told that it's very thick tules and is mostly mud later in the season when the slough level drops.

Marci, who works at the check station recommended searching for a parking lot with a small number of cars and then scouting to find out where the birds are working. This sounds like a good plan to me. Top five ducks harvested as a percentage of total 1986/87 duck harvest: 1. Greenwing teal-30%. 2. Pintail-27%. 3. Mallard-18%. 4. Shoveler-10%. 5. Cinnamon teal-5%. Goose harvest quite small.

Mendota Wildlife Area

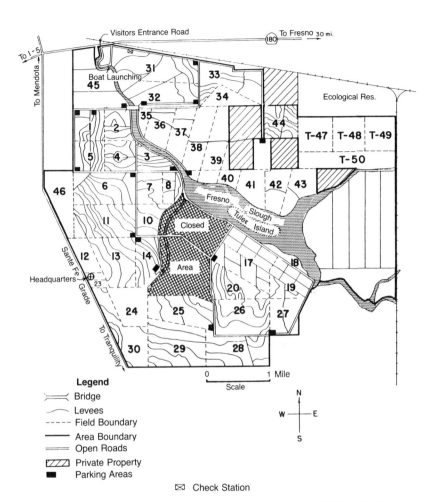

Legend
- Bridge
- Levees
- ----- Field Boundary
- —— Area Boundary
- === Open Roads
- Private Property
- Parking Areas

⊠ Check Station

Reprinted With Permission from the California Department of Fish and Game
Note: These maps are subject to annual revisions. It is important to obtain an up-to-date map
at the refuge, prior to hunting.

Merced National Wildlife Refuge

Size: 1000 acres open to shooting.
Number Of Hunter Allowed: 42 maximum.(When I hunted here in Dec. 86, only 22 hunters were allowed.)
Check In Time: 2 hours before shoot time. Refuge closes at noon.
Trailers: Not allowed.
Boats: Allowed when hunting flooded bypass area.
Hunt Days: Saturday and Wednesday.

Recommendations: Merced is a small refuge with enough barrel blinds to accommodate 22 hunters. This includes two goose blinds. I hunted out of blind number 1 with a hunter from Merced nicknamed Moose. Moose was famous for using a tea kettle lid for a sprig and teal whistle. It worked well on at least one drake sprig. Blind five was the most sought after. In general Merced didn't shoot well in 1986/87.

Late in the season I spoke with a hunter who had done well in one of the goose blinds at Merced while using disposable diapers as decoys. He said that they had put out about one hundred diapers.

Don't get the idea that you have to have reservations to get on the refuge at Merced. I arrived at 4:30 A.M. and got a spot. They don't allow anybody out after shooting time starts. Also keep in mind that the refuge closes at noon. This is one refuge where the hunters aren't allowed to restock shells. If you use up your 25, then you're done for the day. Top four ducks harvested as a percentage of total 1986/87 duck harvest: 1. Greenwing teal-36%. 2. Pintail-20%. 3. Mallard-18%. 4. Shoveler-15%. Hunter success for snow geese was proportionately higher here than any other San Joaquin Valley refuge. Geese killed as a percentage of total ducks and geese harvested: 14%. This is more than ten times the total grassland average for geese and higher than any other valley refuge in 1986/87.

Merced National Wildlife Refuge

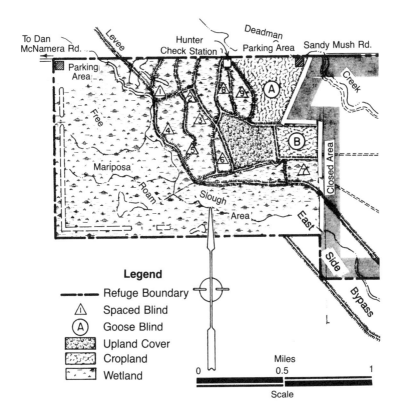

Reprinted With Permission from the California Department of Fish and Game

Note: These maps are subject to annual revisions. It is important to obtain an up-to-date map at the refuge, prior to hunting.

125

Kesterson N. W. R.

Size: 4500 acres open to shooting.*
Hunter Quota: 100*
Check In Time: 2 hours before shoot time.
Boats: Allowed.
Trailers: Allowed.
Shoot Days: Saturday, Sunday, Wednesday.

* Since the closure of area 4 due to high selenium levels these numbers have been reduced considerably. The amount of water available for flooding at Kesterson varies greatly with the amount of rainfall. During early season the number of hunters allowed will generally be quite small. When I hunted here in January of 1987, 58 hunters were allowed entrance.

Recommendations: In 1987 I hunted in the southern end of the windmill complex out of parking lot 3 with my friend Ralph Laughlin. It was the only part of the refuge available when our numbers came up. This was one occasion when early arrival would have helped considerably.

The selenium situation at Kesterson has created a problem. The hazing of ducks in area four is a continuing disturbance and the roar of the propane cannons is annoying. Ralph and I killed four ducks here, but I'd avoid area three until area four is returned to normal again. There are many good barrel blinds in area three.

There are some barrels in the teal lake out of parking lot one that can be excellent. I've had good days here in the past.

The big lake area is a good spot, but very popular, so its hard to get the good locations without reservations and early arrival. This area is reached out of parking lot two.

Top five ducks harvested as a percentage of total 1986/87 duck harvest: 1. Greenwing teal-31%. 2. Mallard-25%. 3. Pintail -13%. 4. Shoveler-10%. 5. Widgeon-5%. Goose harvest quite small.

Kesterson National Wildlife Refuge

Reprinted With Permission from the California Department of Fish and Game
Note: These maps are subject to annual revisions. It is important to obtain an up-to-date map
at the refuge, prior to hunting.

127

Los Banos Wildlife Area

Size: 2700 Acres open to the public.
Hunter Quota: 100
Check In Time: 2 hours before shoot time.
Trailers: Not officially allowed.
Shoot Days: Saturday, Sunday, Wednesday.

Recommendations: Areas 14 through 20 are a substantial walk from parking lot four. I hunted with mixed success on a pond in the northeast corner of area 14. I'd hunt there again. This is a good area to free-lance in and there's plenty of room.

I hunted out of parking lot 5 without much success. This area has several barrels which are good blinds. Its a short walk to the ponds here, but it's close to the spaced blind area so there's always shooting nearby which can prevent birds from working. The spaced blinds are fun to hunt because there's always activity. If the birds are always coming into other blinds first, it can be frustrating. The blinds are right on the edge of the closed zone so birds are constantly in sight. Blinds four, five and six were generally best in 1986/87 according to the Los Banos regulars. If you want to hunt out of a good blind, then its necessary to be near the head of the reservation line; for Sunday shoots it means arriving Friday or early Saturday. (The staff is recommending that reservations be made for Sunday next year so this situation may change.) The reservation line generally got started early Friday due to the popularity of the blinds. Not all of the blinds have good success. It's a good idea to check the kill records for each blind. Some may be low on water. Blinds four, five, six, and twelve were best in 1986/87.

Area 43 on the map is reached from parking lot 7. This area is closed most of the season, but is open for junior hunters and their sponsor on opening weekend, closing weekend and a couple of other days during the season. If interested in hunting this area, it would be best to call the Los Banos headquarters to find out which days it will be open to hunting. I talked with one hunter who had hunted it several times, and he said that it's worth the effort that it takes to get into this area. Top five ducks harvested as a percentage of the total 1986/87 duck harvest: 1. Mallard-27%. 2. Greenwing teal-26%. 3. Pintail-16%. 4. Shoveler-11%. 5. Gadwall-7%.

Los Banos Wildlife Area

Legend
- Permanent & semi-permanent water
- Ditches & sloughs
- Main roads - open to hunters with permit
- Field boundary
- Area boundary
- Parking areas
- Closed zone
- Open to zone 6 permits only
- Open to zone 7 permits only

Scale in miles
0   1/4   1/2   3/4   1 Mile

Reprinted With Permission from the California Department of Fish and Game
Note: These maps are subject to annual revisions. It is important to obtain an up-to-date map at the refuge, prior to hunting.

San Luis National Wildlife Area

Size: 7340 acres total with about 30% open to hunting.
Hunter Quota: 130 maximum.
Time: 2 hours before shoot time.
Trailers: Not allowed.
BOATS: Not allowed.
Hunt Days: Saturday, Sunday, and Wednesday.

Recommendations: If you have reservations, get to the refuge early and hunt out of parking lot 4. This area is surrounded by closed zone and is the most sought after.

I hunted on the northern-most boundary of the refuge and found two barrels there that were taken by other hunters in the morning. After they were vacated, my brother and I took them over and had pretty good activity for mallards in the afternoon. San Luis is a good spot for mallards. For that reason I'd suspect that in general the afternoon shoot here is better than most. Top five ducks harvested as a percentage of total 1986/87 duck harvest: 1. Greenwing teal-46%. 2. Mallard-31%. 3. Shoveler-9%. 4. Pintail-9%. 5. Ringneck-5%. Goose harvest quite small.

San Luis National Wildlife Refuge

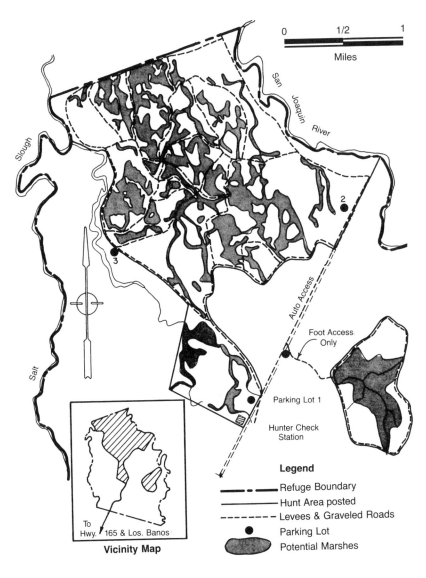

0   1/2   1

Miles

San Joaquin River

Slough

Salt

2

3

Auto Access

Foot Access Only

Parking Lot 1

Hunter Check Station

Legend

— — — Refuge Boundary
———— Hunt Area posted
- - - - - Levees & Graveled Roads
● Parking Lot
Potential Marshes

To Hwy. 165 & Los. Banos

Vicinity Map

Reprinted With Permission from the California Department of Fish and Game
Note: These maps are subject to annual revisions. It is important to obtain an up-to-date map at the refuge, prior to hunting.

Volta Wildlife Area

Size: 2200 acres.
Hunter Quota: 150
Check In Time: Two hours before shoot time.
Trailers: Not allowed.
Boats: Allowed.
HUNT DAYS: Saturday, Sunday and Wednesday.

Recommendations: I hunted in area 10. In general, most of the large tule ponds are good for teal. Larger birds are more selective. Volta is a good place for the first time duck hunter. The main bird here is teal and they tend to be easier to decoy into range than other ducks. The tules provide easy concealment for the hunter. Top five ducks harvested as a percentage of total 1986/87 duck harvest: 1. Greenwing teal-29%. 2. Pintail-17%. 3. Shoveler -12%. 4. Mallard-11%. 5. Cinnamon teal -11%. Three geese were killed in 1986/87.

Volta Wildlife Area

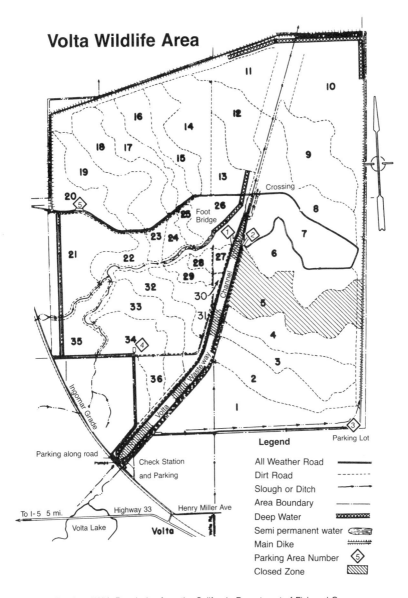

Legend

All Weather Road	——————
Dirt Road	- - - - - - -
Slough or Ditch	•———→
Area Boundary	—·—·—
Deep Water	▓▓▓▓▓
Semi permanent water	⊂═⊃
Main Dike	⊥⊥⊥⊥⊥
Parking Area Number	◇5
Closed Zone	▨

Reprinted With Permission from the California Department of Fish and Game
Note: These maps are subject to annual revisions. It is important to obtain an up-to-date map at the refuge, prior to hunting.

133

Ash Creek Wildlife Area

Size: 9,000 acres open to shooting.
Hunter Quota: Varies with available water and is limited only on opening weekend.
Check In Time: No check station.
Trailers: Not allowed.
Boats: Allowed. No motors.
Hunt Days: Saturday, Sunday and Wednesday.
Type Permit: Type "B" ($25) seasonal use permit or type "A" ($75) seasonal use permit required. No daily permit can be obtained.

Recommendations: This area has lots of potential and is lightly used. It is in an out-of-the way location. The main swamp is a thick tule marsh. Actual waterfowl habitat only covers a small percentage of the refuge. Ash creek itself, which flows through the middle of the valley, forms numerous small ponds which are probably good shooting during the early season.

I hunted here right before the freeze which is a difficult time because the water is covered with ice, but it's too thin to walk on. I was the only hunter on the refuge and quite a few Canada geese passed over early but didn't like my location. I moved closer to the swamp and about 11:00 a.m. a solo honker came to my calling for an easy twenty yard shot.

This refuge is poorly marked. Fortunately, there aren't too many places to go if you make a wrong turn. There are few overnight facilities in the vicinity, and no refuge headquarters to obtain information from. I stayed in Alturas and drove to the refuge for the day. Top six species of ducks and geese as a percentage of 1986/87 total ducks and geese harvested: 1. Mallard-54%. 2. Canada goose-12%. 3. Widgeon-10%. 4. Greenwing teal/Pintail/Gadwall-5% each.

Ash Creek Wildlife Area

Lassen and Modoc Counties

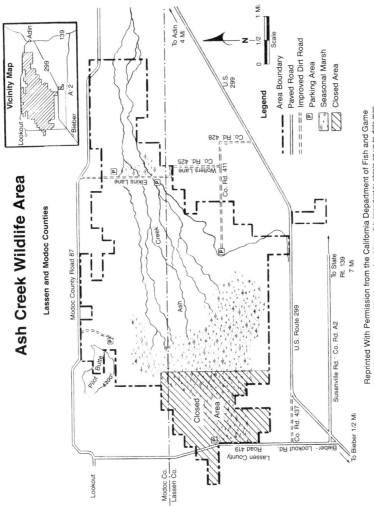

Reprinted With Permission from the California Department of Fish and Game
Note: These maps are subject to annual revisions. It is important to obtain an up-to-date map
at the refuge, prior to hunting.

Butte Valley Wildlife Area

Size: 7,000 acres open to shooting.
Hunter Quota: 38-opening weekend only.
Check In Time: Open two hours before shoot time. No check station.
Trailers: Not allowed.
Boats: Allowed.
Hunt Days: Saturday, Sunday and Wednesday.

Recommendations: This is an excellent spot to hunt honkers. The refuge gets very little activity, so birds work without disturbance.

Recommendations: I walked the refuge and was the only hunter that day. 2,500 acre Meiss Lake has great potential for hunting from layout boats. Also there are islands from which pass shooting opportunity is super. There are about 2,000 acres of seasonal marsh and 3,000 acres of grain land that are greadually flooded as the season progresses. This refuge is just getting started and as time goes by the hunting opportunities will multiply. Top five species of ducks and geese as a percentage of 1986/87 total ducks and geese harvested: 1. Canada goose-22%. 2. Mallard-22%. 3. Widgeon-16%. 4. Greenwing teal-13%. 5. Shoveler-8%.

Butte Valley Wildlife Area

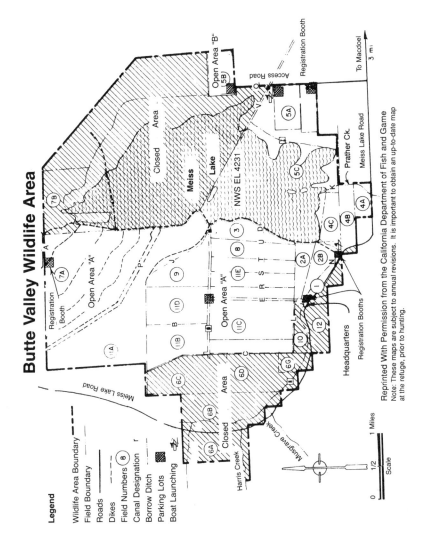

Reprinted With Permission from the California Department of Fish and Game
Note: These maps are subject to annual revisions. It is important to obtain an up-to-date map at the refuge, prior to hunting.

Legend

Wildlife Area Boundary
Field Boundary
Roads
Dikes
Field Numbers ⑧
Canal Designation
Borrow Ditch
Parking Lots
Boat Launching

Honey Lake Wildlife Area

Dakin Unit

Size: 3,500 acres open to shooting.
Hunter Quota: 100. Quota varies with availability of water.
Check In Time: Checking stations are not operated, except on opening weekend of duck and pheasant seasons.
Trailers: Allowed.
Boats: Allowed. No motors.
Shoot Days: Saturday, Sunday and Wednesday.
Permit: Type "A" or "B" season permit required.

Fleming Unit

Size: 2,100 Acres open to shooting.
Hunter Quota: 125. Quota varies with availability of water.
Check In Time: Two hours prior to shooting time.
Trailers: Allowed. This is an excellent spot to bring a trailer.
Boats: Allowed without motors.
Hunt Days: Saturday, Sunday and Wednesday.
Type Permit: Type "B" or "A" season permit.

Recommendations: Honey Lake has traditionally been a good spot to hunt honkers. 1986/87 wasn't up to par in that respect.

Dakin: Field hunting for honkers is popular here. One would have a reasonable chance of shooting a honker by hiding in the sage brush along the lake and pass shooting when the geese get off the water to feed. Ducks and geese tend to "raft up" on the lake, so bad weather is more important here than at some areas. Fleming: I spoke with one hunter who had success using a skull boat on the edge of the lake at the Fleming Unit. The lake has risen and reclaimed some of the ponds along the shoreline.

Percentage of ducks and geese harvested as a percentage of 1986/87 total ducks and geese harvested: 1. Mallard-35%. 2. Widgeon-17%. 3. Canada geese-11%. 4. Gadwall-10%. 5. Pintail-9%. Dakin and Fleming units combined.

Dakin Unit

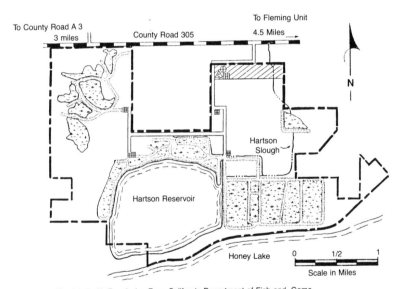

Reprinted with Permission From California Department of Fish and Game

Honey Lake Wildlife Area

Lassen County

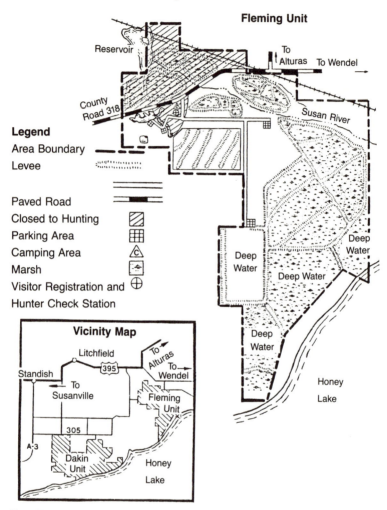

Fleming Unit

Reservoir

To Alturas

To Wendel

County Road 318

Susan River

Legend

Area Boundary

Levee

Paved Road

Closed to Hunting

Parking Area

Camping Area

Marsh

Visitor Registration and
Hunter Check Station

Deep Water

Deep Water

Deep Water

Deep Water

Deep Water

Honey Lake

Vicinity Map

Litchfield

To Alturas

To Wendel

Standish

395

To Susanville

Fleming Unit

305

A-3

Dakin Unit

Honey Lake

Note: These maps are subject to annual revisions. It is important to obtain an up-to-date map at the refuge, prior to hunting.

Lower Klamath National Wildlife Refuge

Size: 47,216 acres total of which approximately 40% is open to waterfowl hunting.
Hunter Quota: Unlimited except for opening day.
Check In Time: Posted at entrance to the refuge. Hunting hours end at 1:00 p.m.
Trailers: Not allowed (see Tule Lake for R.V. park info.)
Boats: Allowed.
Hunt Days: Seven days a week.

Recommendations: Drive the refuge in the afternoon and look for working birds. There is a good chance that they'll still be there in the morning. A boat isn't a must here, but could be helpful in the tule marsh.

Watch for newly flooded areas which can draw feeding ducks. Also watch for mini flyways where ducks fly over hunting areas on their way from one no-hunting zone to another. Right before the freeze ducks will be found around the remaining patches of open water.

Once you're here you may want to get an Oregon license so that you can hunt in the afternoon. It isn't a tremendous extra expense when compared to the overall cost of making the trip. Hunting is allowed until sunset on the Oregon side of the basin.

Reservations are needed to hunt here on opening weekend. Information on how to apply can be obtained by writing the refuge manager.

Top six species of ducks harvested at Tule Lake and Lower Klamath NWR's in 1986/87 as a percentage of total: 1. Mallard-40%. 2. Pintail-23%. 3. Widgeon-14%. 4. Shoveler-8%. 5. Greenwing teal/Gadwall-5%. Geese: 1. Snow-36%. 2. Whitefront-33%. 3. Canada Goose-24%. 4. Ross-6%.

FURTHER INFORMATION: Refuge Manager, Klamath Basin
    National Wildlife Refuges, Route 1 Box 74, Tule Lake,
    CA 96134 Phone: (916) 667-2231

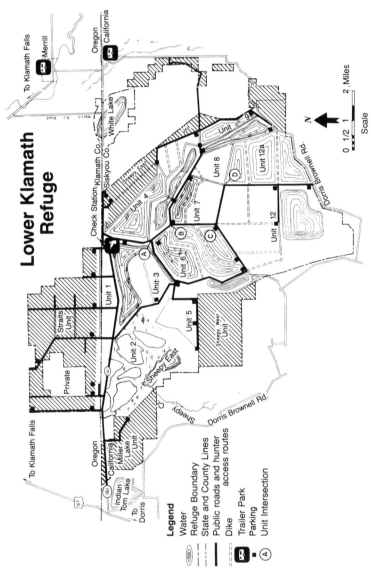

Reprinted With Permission from the United States Fish and Wildlife Service
**Note: Areas open to hunting vary each season. To determine which areas are open to
hunting, contact the refuge manager to obtain an up-to-date map.**

Tule Lake National Wildlife Refuge

Size: 38,980 total acres of which approximately 40% is open to waterfowl hunting.

Hunter Quota: Unlimited after opening weekend.

Check In Time: Posted at entrance to refuge. Hunting hours end at 1:00 p.m.

Trailers: Not allowed. There are five campgrounds in the general vicinity. I stayed at Sheepy Ridge R. V. Park.(916) 667-5370.

Boats: Allowed.

Hunt Days: Every day until 1:00 p.m.

Recommendations: Until the lake freezes over, the marsh is nearly impossible to hunt without a boat. This is a good place to hire a guide to take you out into the marsh. It can be done on your own, but would take some practice to learn the territory. During the first week after the hard freeze of Tule Lake, there's supposed to be great hunting for ducks and geese on the ice.

The spaced blinds can be good for geese. While I was there, a couple days of fog produced good success on snows. There is a drawing each day for blinds so make sure that you arrive early enough to get your shot at the best blinds. The biologist in charge of the drawing will make sure that the best blind locations are included in the draw so you don't have to know the area to have a chance for the good spots. You must have at least one dozen goose decoys to hunt in the spaced blind area. You can call in advance to find out the time of the drawing. The phone number is (916) 667-2231. As with Lower Klamath, Tule Lake requires a permit to hunt on opening weekend. Application procedures can be obtained from the refuge manager.

Top six species of ducks harvested at Tule Lake and Lower Klamath NWR's in 1986/87 as a percentage of total: 1. Mallard-40%. 2. Pintail-23%. 3. Widgeon-14%. 4. Shoveler-

8%. 5. Greenwing teal/Gadwall-5%. Geese: 1. Snow-36%. 2. Whitefront-33%. 3. Canada Goose-24%. 4. Ross-6%.

FURTHER INFORMATION: Refuge Manager, Klamath Basin National Wildlife Refuges, Route 1 Box 74, Tulelake, CA 96134 Phone: (916) 667-2231.

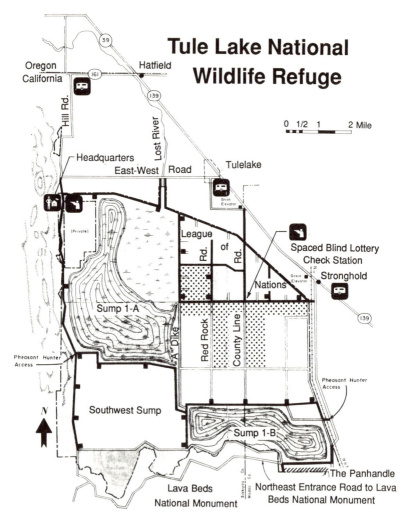

Tule Lake National Wildlife Refuge

Reprinted With Permission from the United States Fish and Wildlife Service

Note: Areas open to hunting, parking areas and check station locations vary each season. To determine which areas are open to hunting, contact the refuge manager to obtain an up-to-date map.

Modoc National Wildlife Refuge

Size: 6,203 acres with 2,130 acres open to shooting.
Hunter Quota: 250 hunters on opening weekend. Unlimited after that.
Check In Time: 90 minutes before shooting time. Check put is required one hour after shooting time is over.
Trailers: Not allowed. There are three RV parks in Alturas. I stayed at DEAN'S R.V. PARK. (916) 233-2066.
Boats: Not allowed.
Shoot Days: Saturday and Sunday on opening weekend. Thereafter Saturday, Tuesday and Thursday.

Recommendations: Scout the area for indications of where the honkers are feeding. Fresh goose pellets are a good sign. Watch for working birds and then set up in that area. Afternoon shoots are good for honkers. I was warned to be careful when wading as there is deep water in unexpected places.

Traditionally reservations for opening weekend at Modoc have been accepted August 1-15. Detailed instructions explaining the application proceedure can be obtained from the refuge manager. In the past, hunters who applied for permits on the Modoc National Wildlife Refuge could not apply for the Tule Lake or Lower Klamath hunts. I imagine that this rule will continue.

FURTHER INFORMATION: Refuge Manager, Modoc National Wildlife Refuge, P.O. Box 1610, Alturas, CA 96101
Phone:(916) 233-3572

145

Modoc National Wildlife Refuge

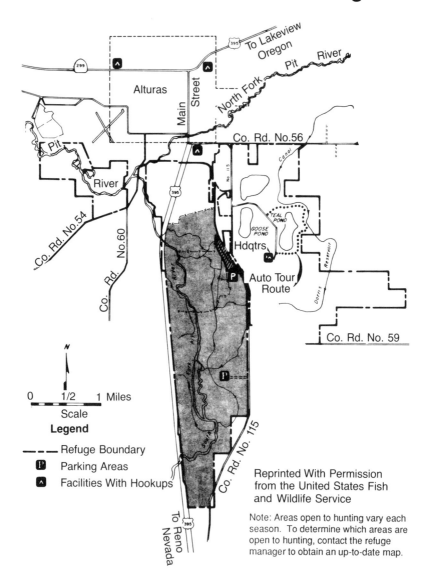

Reprinted With Permission
from the United States Fish
and Wildlife Service

Note: Areas open to hunting vary each
season. To determine which areas are
open to hunting, contact the refuge
manager to obtain an up-to-date map.

146

Resources

Pac 'orse Systems
606 N.W. 94th St.
Vancouver, WA 98665
(206) 574-1999
The Pac 'orse is a one wheel deer carrier that can also be used for hauling duck decoys. Using the above phone number the manufacturer can be contacted directly.

J&J Manufacturing
P.O. Box 7334
San Jose, CA 95150
(408) 559-0372
The Duck Truck is a decoy cart that floats, allowing you to tow it right into the pond.

Iverson Game Bird Calls
P.O. Box 917
Novato, CA 94948
(415) 897-9179
Many people can't justify the price of an Iverson call, but for me it's the first call that I've been able to keep in good working order for several seasons without replacing it.

Plasti-Duck
6707 Airway Dr.
Klamath Falls, OR 97603
(503) 882-7702
Plasti-Duck still makes the inflatable decoys that I consider to be ideal for refuge hunting. They deflate so that you can fit an extra half dozen into your pack. They're very durable too, I've had mine since 1972 and they're going strong.

Harry Boyle
#4 Nicole Lane
Chico, CA 95926
(916) 342-0617
Instructional tapes.

Billy Gianquinto
5726 Hall Rd.
Santa Rosa, CA 95401
(707) 526-6505
Instructional tapes.

BENIK CORP.
8169 Tracyton Blvd. NW
Bremerton, WA 98310
(206) 692-5601
Manufacturer of neoprene waders.

STATE OF CALIFORNIA DEPARTMENT OF FISH AND GAME
1416 Ninth St.
Sacramento, CA 95816
(916) 846-3315
Ask for Dan Connelly. Dan is at the hub of policy making
decisions at the state level.

Dennis Ludington
14999 Volta Rd.
Los Banos, CA 93635
(209) 826-0618
Dennis is a professional dog trainer and guide.

California Waterfowl Association
Dan Chapin
3840 Rosin Ct., Suite #100
Sacramento, CA 95834

Ducks Unlimited
Jerry C. Cawthon, Regional Director
P.O. Box 1311
Los Banos, CA 93635
(209) 826-3394

Ray Burmaster
8325 La Riviera Dr.
Sacramento, CA 95826
(916) 383-7235
Ray is a member of the Sacramento Valley Waterfowl Committee and represents the unaffiliated hunters.

Paul Kinsyon Duck Calls
607 N. 5th St.
Burlington, Iowa 52601
(319) 752-4465
Dennis Ludington recommends this call. He likes it because
it sounds good, is easy to blow, and comes permanently
tuned.

Refuge Addresses

Butte Valley Wildlife Area
Manager: Gordon Asheraft
P.O. Box 249
Macdoel, CA 96058

Colusa National Wildlife
Refuge
Check with Sacramento
headquarters.

Delevan National Wildlife
Refuge
Check with Sacramento
headquarters.

Gray Lodge Wildlife Area
Manager: R.B. Reno
P.O. Box 37
Gridley, CA 95948

Grizzly Island Wildlife Area
Manager: Dennis Becker
2548 Grizzly Island Rd.
Suisun, CA 94585

Honey Lake Wildlife Area
Manager: Robert Weld
Wendel, CA 96136

Kesterson National Wildlife
Refuge
Check with San Luis National
Wildlife Refuge headquarters.

Klamath Basin National
Wildlife Refuges
Manager: Roger Johnson
Rt.1 Box 74
Tulelake, CA 96134

Los Banos Wildlife Area
Manager: Pete Blake
18110 West Henry Miller Ave.
Los Banos, CA 93635

Mendota Wildlife Area
Manager: Bob Huddleston
P.O. Box 37
Mendota, CA 93640

Merced National Wildlife
Refuge
Check with San Luis National
Wildlife Refuge headquarters.

Modoc National Wildlife
Refuge
Manager: E. Clark Bloom
P.O. Box 1610
Alturas, CA 96101

Sacramento National Wildlife
Refuge
Manager: Edward Collins
Rt.1 Box 311
Willows, CA 95988

San Luis National Wildlife
Refuge
Manager: Gary Zahm
P.O. Box 2176
Los Banos, CA 93635

Sutter National Wildlife
Refuge
Check with Sacramento
headquarters.

Volta Wildlife Area
Manager: Pete Blake
18110 West Henry Miller Ave.
Los Banos, CA 93635

Index

152

ORDER FORM

MAIL TO:

Towhee Publishing
P.O.Box 8500
Suite #169
Danville, California 94526

Please send me ___ copy(ies) of
Hunting Ducks and Geese @ $13.95 each _____

* California only $.91	* Sales tax _____
** $1.50 for first book, $.75 for each additional book.	** Shipping _____ or *** UPS _____
*** I can't wait 4-6 weeks for Book Rate. Here's $3.00 for United Parcel Service.	

Total enclosed _____

Name _____

Address _____

City/State _____ Zip _____

I understand that I may return the book for a full refund if not satisfied. Please wait 4-6 weeks for delivery.